PRAISE FOR *A CULTURE OF PROMISE*

Author and business leader Fee Stubblefield has created both a business model and a life model to encourage common sense for the common good. To read *A Culture of Promise* is to open one's mind and heart to a world of compassionate service and quality outcomes for senior living.

—Barbara T. Roberts
Governor of Oregon 1991-1995
Resides at The Springs Living

"Promise not to put me in an old folks' home." Keeping that promise and knowing that customers will not put up with the same old practices that led to that plea has inspired Fee Stubblefield on a quest to transform what we offer in senior living. The insights he shares in *A Culture of Promise* are essential reading for every provider, entrepreneur, and investor in the industry. Read this book both to understand and to deliver on the promises you make as an operator to your customers, your employees, and your capital partners.

—Bob Kramer
Founder and Fellow, Nexus Insights
Cofounder and Strategic Advisor, NIC

A Culture of Promise is a great read for any operator committed to improving their quality of care. Fee has achieved scale with a quality operation. Very few in our sector have done that. He reveals the specific quality and financial measures he focuses on that have led to his success. The book is a template for all who want to provide great care and grow at the same time.

—Mark Parkinson
Governor of Kansas 2009-2011
President & CEO of American Health Care Association (AHCA)

With *A Culture of Promise*, Fee offers leaders an essential and heartfelt guide to extreme ownership and impact in business. You may see elements of yourself in these pages.

—Kelsey Mellard
Founder and CEO, Sitka

Fee Stubblefield writes about "caring" as one of the main components for success. Having been a friend of, and investor with, Stubblefield for over a dozen years, and having toured his communities by his side, it is obvious that "caring" is not merely something to write in a book or business mission statement. "Caring" is demonstrated face to face. Going through a Springs Living community with Fee is like being on tour with a rock star. Residents approach him from all over the rooms with big smiles on their faces, and he reciprocates with a genuine outpouring of affection. The key to success is not reading this book but living it out on a daily basis.

—Wayne Tatusko, Esquire
Tatusko Law

A Culture of Promise is an innovative and thought-provoking challenge to all long-term care (LTC) providers and policy makers. Fee Stubblefield uniquely defines the issues that consumers and providers face. Demonstrating how even the well-intended can unintentionally contribute to the systemic problems that have been created. Mr. Stubblefield has developed a new paradigm for how our US LTC system can achieve better outcomes for all stakeholders.

This book will force us all to reexamine our philosophies and beliefs about how we do what we do. And open our minds to a different model that balances the needs of all who work, live, and service the LTC ecosystem. This is a must read that you will have a hard time putting down.

—Phil Fogg, Jr.
CEO of Marquis Companies

An important book for anyone who wants to thrive in the later stages of adulthood. Fee's journey and the culture he has created in his company provide keen insights and direction for people who want to live and age with purpose and direction (not to mention have a little fun along the way). Understanding the natural changes that occur as we age is critical to guiding us all along our own journey.

—Jim Carlson
Retired CEO and President
Oregon Health Care Association

Good leaders provide direction, purpose, culture, and mission for a group or organization to follow. They also share their knowledge, wisdom, and experience with others. Their leadership becomes a calling to serve others. Fee Stubblefield is a dynamic and successful entrepreneur who has risen to his position in the industry through both actions and words. Fee's thought leadership on culture, alignment, and purpose are clear, specific, and on target in today's changed senior living landscape.

—Kurt C. Read
Partner, RSF Partners

A Culture of Promise weaves a personal life journey with a thoughtful approach to the business of caring for older adults. Fee's insights provide food for thought for professionals in the senior housing industry and a helpful perspective for all of us on the aging journey. A timely book as we begin meeting the needs and wants of millions of Baby Boomers.

—Ray Braun
President and CEO
National Investment Center for Seniors Housing and Care (NIC)

Quality and performance metrics are critical to support growth in the rapidly developing industry of caring for older adults—for the residents and staff as well as for those providing capital to the industry. In *A Culture of Promise,* Stubblefield expertly identifies tangible metrics to measure quality of care, a must-have measurement for navigating operational excellence, resident and staff quality of life and experience, and evolving aspirational goals with practical outcomes. Recognizing company culture and limitations on achievable and realistic growth, Stubblefield provides a thought-provoking book for business leaders to consider as they grow their businesses in the societally important and critical senior care industry.

—Beth Burnham Mace
Former Chief Economist and Director of Research & Analytics
National Investment Center for Senior Housing and Care (NIC)

a Culture of Promise

a Culture of Promise

THE TRUE STORY OF
A SMALL COMPANY'S QUEST
TO TRANSFORM THE
SENIOR LIVING INDUSTRY

FEE STUBBLEFIELD

Forbes | Books

Published by Forbes Books, Charleston, South Carolina.
An imprint of Advantage Media Group.

Forbes Books is a registered trademark, and the Forbes Books colophon is a trademark of Forbes Media, LLC.

Printed in the United States of America.

10 9 8 7 6 5 4 3 2 1

ISBN: 979-8-88750-315-8 (Hardcover)
ISBN: 979-8-88750-316-5 (eBook)

Library of Congress Control Number: 2024902306

Cover design by Matthew Morse.
Layout design by Ruthie Wood.

Since 1917, Forbes has remained steadfast in its mission to serve as the defining voice of entrepreneurial capitalism. Forbes Books, launched in 2016 through a partnership with Advantage Media, furthers that aim by helping business and thought leaders bring their stories, passion, and knowledge to the forefront in custom books. Opinions expressed by Forbes Books authors are their own. To be considered for publication, please visit books.Forbes.com.

To my grandmothers, Lillian Stubblefield and Esther Short, without whom my life would have taken a different direction.

To my mom, who gave me the fire to do hard things, and to my life partner, Julie, who has pushed me to walk introspectively in the world.

This book is also dedicated to everyone who has helped me along the way, including those who did not make building a company easy, and especially my colleagues who directly care for the families we serve.

CONTENTS

INTRODUCTION

Some people blaze a path through your life. My grandmother Lillian was one of those people—imprinted on my heart forever. *Promise Not to Put Me in an Old Folks' Home* was the title I really wanted for this book. Those were my grandmother's exact words many years ago. You may have even heard this phrase (or some variation) from your parents or your grandparents, or you may have even thought this for yourself.

For us all, I think living a great, *active* life for a long time is the goal. Do you have life goals, like having a rewarding job or business where you do well financially and are a part of something bigger than yourself and where you experience meaningful relationships … all to someday grow older and retire? If so, you may find yourself at the end of that great life saying "Promise not to put me in an old folks' home!"

I don't want that to happen to me, to my grandmother, or to you, and that is why I wrote this book.

As I worked with the folks at Forbes Books, we finally agreed to call this book *A Culture of Promise,* not because it's better for the search algorithms or because the URL was available (though it is and it was) but because it was a promise that started this whole grand adventure. This book will introduce you to a new kind of promise, an aspirational promise, which, ironically, is a promise that cannot be kept. Well, actually, there is one way to fulfill an aspirational promise, but we will cover that later in the book. Aspirational promises always fail but are a key ingredient in the creation of organizational culture, and organizational culture is the key to success because we work with other people, no matter what business sector we are in. When you have more than one person, you have culture; therefore, as your culture goes, so goes your company. And so, we called this book *A Culture of Promise* because it's about an aspirational promise, but it's also about an industry that has an important and promising future.

The True Story of a Small Company's Quest to Transform the Senior Living Industry makes me a little uncomfortable. Probably because it could be taken wrongly, as if I believe it is only my company that has been passionate about changing the industry.

I do not believe that.

We are just one of many organizations working passionately to make a difference.

It's our customers themselves who are demanding change because they will not put up with the same old practices that created that phrase "Promise not to put me in an old folks' home." If we listen, we will hear their pleas for quality, dignity, respect, and affordability. As a whole, the senior housing and care industry is reeling after COVID-19. Today, many organizations are dealing with what I call "long COVID-19 business impacts" like workforce issues, quality problems, and cost increases, the most significant being rising interest rates. A lack of capital to expand and invest in our businesses is happening at the same time that over 73 million baby boomers are getting ready to need our services.[1] Now is the time for us to have a frank conversation about the relationship between organizational quality and growth and what business we are really in. COVID-19

---

1   "2020 Census Will Help Policymakers Prepare for the Incoming Wave of Aging Boomers," Census.gov, December 10, 2019, https://www.census.gov/library/stories/2019/12/by-2030-all-baby-boomers-will-be-age-65-or-older.html.

has taken much from us, but it has also provided a historic opportunity for change. It is my prediction that those organizations, both for profit and not for profit, that are in the real estate business (what I call companies who buy up properties but are not mission focused on caring for the people) will struggle to survive in the great boomer influx into senior housing and care ahead.

If we can restore trust and quality for our customers by working collaboratively to fulfill our industry promises to our workforce, we will be like the rising phoenix and soar to new and high places. Not just financial high places, but places of high quality. Quality must come first for all older adults, whether they need affordable housing and care, are trapped in the no-man's-land of the middle market, or have the privilege to live in the highest-quality communities. Every older adult should have high quality, but don't confuse high quality with the physical building or gourmet food; think of high-quality care, support, and love designed for every budget. One of the biggest fears most older adults have is outliving their money. To achieve our societal goals on the care of our seniors, we must work with all the stakeholders, governmental regulators, and yes, even politicians. We must look at each resident as someone we love deeply, like my grandmother—just as we would want others to do for us.

Let's start with that, then build backward toward the real estate and financial returns. Let's be growers of quality who plant orchards of golden apples, not scalers with machines stamping out widgets. Let's act like guardians of our galaxy and fulfill our promises of quality support and care. Quality support and care does not mean problems won't happen and that no one will ever fall or die, because they will. Quality is how we deal with those problems when the inevitable happens in someone's life. And so, I guess I am OK with the punchy subtitle. Hopefully, it will get more people to open this book, because sometimes, to make change, we need to make ourselves and others a little uncomfortable.

The Springs Living, the company I founded in 1996—along with our peers, our partners in capital, insurance, healthcare, and other services—is up to meeting the challenge of the great boom ahead. We are standing on the shoulders but also the ashes of many innovative and smart organizations and people who have come before us. Let's look for guidance in their examples—the successes but especially the failures, where the ghosts of organizations once at the top failed to deliver on their promises. In these pages, I will tell you what has worked for our organization and what I believe will work for any organization. I will also offer my thoughts on the future and how we get there. My hope is that this book is entertaining, but more than that, I hope that I have done justice to a true story. Maybe this book will connect some dots for you, as it has for me, and lead us both to change the world together.

For Those of You with an Entrepreneurial Heart

I always knew I wanted to run my own business. I just didn't realize the crazy journey that dream would take me on. As a child, I remember floating on an inner tube in the pool at Lehman Hot Springs, the place where I grew up, thinking of all the ways I would improve it someday. It was the family resort my grandfather and grandmother purchased in 1925. I expected to run that business after my grandfather and dad, but fate had a different plan after our family lost everything and went bankrupt in 1988.

I am still surprised by the business I started and now run, The Springs Living, because I didn't even know senior housing and care could be a business. All I set out to do was solve a problem for someone I loved very much, my grandmother. It turned out that that desire, mixed with skills and experience I developed along the way, strategy, and a lot of help from great people with whom I share similar values, has created something pretty special. Equally, if you have an interest in starting and growing a business or organization, either for profit or not for profit, this is a book you will want to read. Those of you who do not feel "qualified" to own and start a business but still long to will be especially interested in my journey. It's a true story that will demonstrate what can happen when we follow our heart, our calling, our purpose, or whatever you want to call it. After turning the manuscript in to the editor at Forbes Books, I had a feeling much like I imagined a near-death experience would be. Rereading the book was like the out-of-body experience we hear about when people die. Looking down at the completed manuscript, I wondered where the time had gone and how this story had all happened. But I also feel an excitement about what is next in my future filled with hope and potential.

If you are someone who has parents or grandparents or are planning on being old at some point in your life, you will want to read this—no, you *need* to read this. The experiences and insights are universal and the perspectives necessary to continue the changes that are happening even now. I believe this book holds concepts that can help any business but will especially help lead the senior housing and care industry into the great boom ahead.

CHAPTER 1

It Starts with a Promise

Promises are only as strong as the people who give them.

–Stephen Richards

"Promise to never put me in an old folks' home," Lillian said with conviction and intent. Her eyes looked directly at me as if they could see the future.

"Of course, Grandma," I reassured her.

"I just want to stay in my own home," she said, the emphasis in her voice pushing the stakes higher.

"I understand," I said, my pitch falling away as I dug back into my memory of the first time I had heard her plea.

The first time was in 1975. I was ten years old, just old enough for memories to fix in my mind about my first experience of going to a nursing home. Grandma and I climbed into her 1972 white Ford LTD sedan. As she turned the key and as the big Cleveland engine roared to life, she said, "Before we go to the post office, we are going to stop by and see a friend of mine in the nursing home." I was staying the night at Grandma's house, as I often did. I loved staying at her house, not just because she had a TV, which we did not have at our house, but because I truly enjoyed being around her and tagging along as she ran the day's errands.

We drove north, out of Pendleton, Oregon, toward Mission, the little town located on the local reservation. I enjoyed the drive up the Umatilla River and into a part of town I didn't often go to. She parked the car, and we got out. I followed her up the narrow concrete sidewalk to the nondescript one-story nursing home just outside town. Not finding anyone at the front desk, she turned right down a long linoleum hallway buzzing with fluorescent light. We took another right and went to the end of the hall. The room was dark, and I stopped at the doorway.

The elderly woman's eyes lit up as we walked into the room. She pointed to a single chair in the corner of the sparsely furnished room, indicating I should sit there. As I watched my grandmother hold the lady's hand, she cocked her head to the right and began speaking in warm, hushed tones.

As they talked, their mannerisms conveyed understanding and empathy, and the conversation seemed heartfelt and resigned. Even at that young age, I got the feeling that this was the last time they would hold each other's hands ... and they knew it. Eventually, Grandma glanced back at me, indicating it was time to leave, bent and kissed her friend softly on the forehead, and silently walked out of the room, holding out her hand as a gesture for me to follow.

We hadn't gone but a few steps when she stopped and glanced to her right into another room. She backed up and this time looked back down the hallway in both directions as if looking for something or someone. No one was there. She entered the room. Once again, I waited at the door, but this time she didn't indicate that I should follow.

On the bed was a scene that would sear into my young memory. Forgotten, a man lay naked, partially in the fetal position, exposed, alone, and seemingly irrelevant. His arms were hugging his worn and aged body, and his dignity, his story, and his name read only "Room 34." No name or indication of the humanity inside was visible.

This was my first glimpse into the world of long-term care, a nursing home that favored numbers and tasks above dignity, autonomy, and caring for people. Not that the people working there didn't care; I never believed that to be the case. They were doing their best in a system that society, politics, and bureaucracy created in a very different time in history. A well-intentioned system had evolved more into the warehousing of people society did not consider useful. Maybe a practical decision of the times, it had devolved humanity into numbers, dollars, and boxes to check so that companies could get their payments from the government. It was as if we had hidden the value of our older adults' humanity. In front of each room, patient, and person was a name forgotten, and it felt wrong.

My grandmother went to the gentleman and gently replaced the sheet and blanket that had fallen on the floor. Tucking him in, like she used to do with me when I was a young boy, she touched his shoulder and whispered words I could not hear. Her brief actions were full of humanity and love even though she did not know this man. In hindsight, I now understand that her actions also communicated an understanding that if this could happen to this man, it could happen to her.

Even today when I remember that moment, I get a lump in my throat and have to hold back a physical reaction that borders on tears. The tears are a mix of sadness and that deep love you feel for those you aren't able to hold anymore. But I also felt determination, if that can be an emotion. Determination to not let that happen to someone I love or even to myself. The experience burned into me a deep sense of right and wrong, and no matter how well intentioned this nursing home was, it was wrong. It could be, and should be, better. Grandma drove the powerful Ford away from the nursing home like she was escaping her future, and that was the first time I heard her say *"Promise to never put me in an old folks' home."*

The Second Time

The second time I heard Lillian say, "I don't want to go to an old folks' home—I just want to stay in my own home" was in the hospital right after she had a heart attack. Twenty years had passed, and now Lillian was in her mideighties. Most of us age slowly, and then one day something happens: the body breaks.

A familiar story for many families, ours gathered outside the room to discuss next steps. Moving her to a retirement community was not an option. We ended up taking her home. When she returned from the hospital, she would sit in her old dark-green recliner patterned with textured flowers, in early-1970s style. Recovering from a heart attack was harder on her than the heart attack itself. The doctors ordered her to take it easy, an unseen restraint. She was always fiercely independent, active, and self-reliant, but now her beloved chair had become her prison. The family took turns staying with her, mowing the lawn, shopping, and, of course, trying to manage the many pills her doctors insisted she take.

As my mom, dad, and aunt considered options, I thought about my promises to Lillian—and the roots of our family's story and the promises woven through it.

Roots of a Promise

"Lax-ayxpa" … I can still hear the throaty pronunciation of the ancient Cayuse word. "Lax-ayxpa," he repeated. "La WAIF pah," he pronounced slower so I could understand and repeat. Chief Jesse Jones stood beside the hot stream of mineral water that flowed out of the ground as he waved his outstretched hand, palm down, in a sweeping motion over the sacred ground in front of him. "This is a special place for my people," he said.

"*Lax-ayxpa* is what my people called this place. It means 'hot place,'" he said with the distinctive accent of the local Native Americans I grew up hearing my whole life.

The film crew was just setting up, and Jesse and I had started talking before the mic was live and the camera rolling. The director Maya's eyes widened—she looked like she had missed the opportunity of a lifetime. This was the first time Jesse had been to Lehman Hot Springs since he was a young man. Now in his late seventies, he had agreed to come to the source and tell the old story of Lax-ayxpa.

The old story began before James Lehman had filed a Donation Land Claim in 1878 and turned Lax-ayxpa into Lehman Hot Springs, a turn-of-the-century wellness resort for Oregon Trail travelers and settlers. It was the story of the place before local ranchers turned the fertile grassland into wheat ground and started running cattle and sheep through the mountains. It was the story before my grandfather, Fancho Stubblefield, who was born on a homestead not far from Lehman in 1898, purchased the resort in 1925 with a dream to make Lehman Hot Springs into a legacy.

Origin Story

Lehman Hot Springs was our family business, a small resort located on five hundred acres. Deep in the Blue Mountains near Pendleton, Oregon. I am not sure if the magic it held in my life was because of the physical place itself, a natural hot mineral springs where fifty artesian springs emerge from the ground to fill soaking and swimming pools for visitors under majestic, towering ponderosa pines and tamarack trees, or if it was that our family had lived and worked here for four generations. Most of those generations felt more like we were serving the land than it was serving us. Life was not easy, but we took pride in being able to do hard things.

From where the resort sits halfway up a canyon, the waters flow north down Warm Springs Creek, then Camas Creek, the John Day River, and eventually the Columbia River. Lehman's mineral water finally meets the Pacific Ocean after an almost five-hundred-mile journey. Long-cooled and mixed with every spring, creek, and river in the Pacific Northwest, its minerals add to the whole and seem insignificant in the world, yet they are not.

At the source, the natural mineral water emerges from the ground at 150 degrees Fahrenheit and flows into the soaking and swimming pools. There, it pauses to entertain, delight, and heal its guests. But, as in all things limited by time, it has to continue its journey by flowing out of the pools and into the basin, which will be its future. The water came from this magical place, and so did I, but like those bubbling hot springs, I also had been swept away from that place and into an uncertain future.

Modern-day Lehman Hot Springs pools in the early morning.

A Promise for Lillian

Shaking off my memories of the past, I rejoined the urgent, hushed conversation among our family. How were we going to keep our grandma in her own home? Something was stirring inside me. It was like the feeling of an unseen person being in a room with you—a feeling I could not shake off. Something was brewing. That childhood promise had taken root, and although I still had no idea how to fulfill the promise, I had a sixth sense that there was a way. At the moment, there was not much I could do other than agree to fulfill the set of chores assigned and wait.

"We take care of our own" was the family's theme. Each of us had our duties, and mine was to help with the lawn, errands, and chores. Lillian always loved a great lawn and spent much of her life tending to its care as if it were a dependent child. My mother and aunt would share scheduling and taking her to doctors' appointments as well as managing her medications and helping with more personal needs like showers. The men would do the handyman stuff and help other family members drive her to the store to shop for groceries. We had a plan, and she would stay in her own home. We all knew this would be a temporary solution.

And we were but one family among literally countless others facing these same difficult choices.

CHAPTER 2

Why Make a Promise?

It makes my heart sick when I remember all the good words and the broken promises.

—Chief Joseph

Why did my grandmother say "Promise not to put me in an old folks' home," and why does that statement resonate with so many people who wholeheartedly agree? Why didn't she say "Promise to care for me when I can't do it for myself" or "I just want to live in a good place surrounded by people who are kind and competent"? Her statement was negative, fear based, and discriminatory. She was none of those things. Not only was she communicating her opinion of the long-term care industry; she was reflecting the opinion of the general population, and that opinion is still deeply held by many, if not most, older adults.

However, she was also grappling with human nature—*her* human nature. That realization that we will not live forever and that this world will end. Like when, as little kids on the playground for the first time, our friend pushes us from behind down the slide before we are ready. Maybe it is like that moment of fear before we become resigned to the inevitable?

"Old folks." No one wants to be an old folk, even if you are a hundred years old, because of what that statement really means. It means that people will treat us like children, our autonomy and dignity fading. Pejoratively they disregard our contributions because we are closer to the end of our life than the beginning. It means we aren't an individual, Lillian Stubblefield or Joe Biden, but rather an old person. Her point was that something was missing.

She kept two large magnets, three to four inches long, on a shelf beside her recliner. As a kid, I would play with those magnets while she sat watching *Days of Our Lives* or *General Hospital*, popular soap operas of the 1970s and 1980s. I was fascinated by the magnets because I could never get the two positive ends to touch each other. No matter what I tried, one would repulse the other, never to touch. Looking back, I think maybe those magnets offer a metaphor for what we have created in our long-term care system. No one wants to move into an old folks' home. It's as if we are trying to care for folks with the same two ends of the magnet. They need to go, but they don't want to—negative and negative.

Yet when I would turn one end of one of the magnets around, the positive end and the negative end would almost slam together to make a strong connection. If you didn't get your finger out of the way, you might lose a fingernail—it was such a strong attraction. It's simply a natural principle of electromagnetism. What if the senior living profession could improve by the recognition of this natural principle? Why can't we add the positive to what is perceived to be a negative phase of life? What if we can figure out how to create and care for people in environments that they *want* to move into? Like a cold glass of water on a hot day, moving to more supportive living should be a relief to the individual and their family and friends, not the worst moment of their life.

Instead of repelling people, we can align with what they want and need in order to create something strong and magnetic. We can construct environments of support where people can't wait to get old enough to move in. Why can't we change the paradigm? What if we build communities and services that make life just a little easier and better for older adults? What if our system satisfies a need for connection and safety and creates quality in life? I contend that rethinking the environments we create can offer profound hope and cause people to be relieved to move to a more supportive environment where the chores are done for you and you can focus on the important things in life like relationships. When I say recreating environments, I don't mean redesigning buildings. I mean recreating the entire life-stage experience. Combine inviting physical spaces with opportunities to understand and enhance our whole person's physical, psychological, and spiritual needs.

The 1960s long-term care system was created by well-meaning people who were younger and healthier than the people moving in. It was an early attempt at solving a problem and, while well-intended, we didn't get it right. Like I had promised my grandmother not to put her in an old folks' home, the nursing home industry had made a promise to seniors too—to take care of them. This well-intentioned goal by politicians and regulators and company executives started with great expectations, but somewhere along the way it was rejected by those it intended to serve. That rejection because of the quality was the seed that my grandmother planted in my heart and mind.

The Safe Promise: The Skilled Nursing Home Era

Bob Kramer, cofounder of the National Investment Center, a nonprofit dedicated to research, innovation, and connecting capital to the senior housing and care industry, classified this period beginning in the 1960s and ending in the early 1990s as the Skilled Nursing Home period. Its goal and "promise" were to keep folks safe. Keeping folks safe is what we want to do for other people. We care, so we put bumper guards on corners, create restraints so people can't fall out of bed, and feed them nutritionally balanced meals that taste like eating a newspaper—but we kept them safe. But safety is not what we want primarily for ourselves—safety is the only part of the promise.

My grandmother saw what only focusing on safety looked like, and she didn't want anything to do with it. While we want ourselves and others to be safe, what we want for ourselves is to be free to make our own decisions in life. As we age, we still want the autonomy to make our own choices—at least until we are not capable any longer. The reason the skilled nursing industry failed in its first attempt was that it focused too much on safety over autonomy. Anytime you have one party paying the bills, the government, while a third party is your customer, it's really hard to make the third party satisfied. This is the United States of America, land of the brave and home of the free. We simply want to be free to live our lives any way we choose.

In our society, we work our entire lives so that one day we have the resources to retire, thumb our noses at "the man," and ride off into the ultimate freedom of retirement. Many of the Eisenhower Generation and Silent Generation didn't work hard for decades in jobs they weren't passionate about just to lose their freedoms in their later years.

However, for many it has not worked out that way. First, the economics of retirement leave us fearing we will run out of money before we run out of life. Today, 56 percent of people say they are not on track to retire comfortably.[2] Those jobs that offered pensions to make retirement affordable have declined—and people move jobs more frequently. The world is different from the world where you worked a job until you were sixty-five, got a gold watch, and went off into the sunset.

The Assisted Living Era

Keren Brown Wilson, considered by many as the modern-day founder of assisted living in the United States, pointed out in the mid-1990s in her book *Assisted Living: Reconceptualizing Regulation to Meet Consumers' Needs & Preferences* the idea I just discussed: what we want for others is that they be safe and cared for, but what we want for ourselves is autonomy, the ability to live life the way we choose. (And if we could maintain our lifestyle, so much the better.) Safety for someone in the last part of their life is complicated, and the spirit wants to experience life. That is hard to do if safety is your only focus. The promise needed to change.

What I have observed is that when you get older, you realize the value of every moment and want to make your own determination of safety. You want to live. Of course, you can keep someone from falling if you tie them to a bed, and that is exactly what the system allowed in the nursing home era. But that is not what the human

---

2   Kamaron McNair, "56% of Americans Say They're Not on Track to Comfortably Retire: How to Catch Up," September 8, 2023, https://www.cnbc.com/2023/09/08/56percent-of-americans-say-theyre-not-on-track-to-comfortably-retire.html.

spirit wants. It's not what my grandmother wanted, and it's not what anyone would want for their life.

Bob Kramer explains that the second generation of senior housing started in the 1990s and continued until March of 2020. It ushered in new concepts, capital, and developments to make it better. Here, we attempted to evolve the old nursing home into a better building and a lower cost, and the emphasis became a social model. This era was focused on building real estate that would offer a homelike environment with choice and autonomy. Organizations expanded rapidly and significantly improved the quality of living for older adults.

Like each version of new software, we did improve, but huge glitches remained. The real estate was built significantly better, more homelike, and was not a "one-size-fits-all" concept. Based on a social and not a medical model, community-based care or senior housing and care evolved with the customer. Not only was this social concept more physically inviting; it was more affordable. Gone was the excessive governmental cost and compliance of skilled nursing. Assisted living allowed for people to live in a nicer place and at a cost that addressed their fear of running out of money and being on the government dime.

For the Depression-era relatives I grew up with, like my grandmother, not being dependent on the government was just as motivating as not running out of money. They had seen the mass inefficiency when the government controlled a thing and harbored a generational value not to be reliant on a controlled bureaucracy, and assisted living was an answer. Yet we saw problems emerge, as it was often treated as a real estate play, and the service component had big gaps in quality with little consistency for the customer.

We overcorrected by fleeing the model of a nursing home and creating a more homelike environment—with almost no professional service. Hospitality became many organizations' focus as the industry tried to mimic what the hotel industry had successfully created. The only problem is that the senior housing industry is much different than the hospitality industry. To say that senior housing is hospitality is like saying that hospitality is real estate. Yes, hospitality is an important component of senior housing, but it is not the driver. We are in the service industry, with hospitality, like real estate, just one component. It was in this second era, the assisted living era, that The Springs Living was born. I remember that our first building didn't even have a LPN or RN on staff but had only twenty hours of contract RN nursing per week! Today that is unimaginable, as the needs have grown; that same community now has two full-time RNs. In every way, we have evolved, grown, learned, and remained committed to providing a place and community where our residents and all those who work for us feel at home.

Our New Era: Postpandemic Model

In March of 2020, the assisted living era ended abruptly, like a door being slammed in our collective face. The COVID-19 pandemic was like a tsunami, leveling organizational structures and organizations themselves and returning the landscape to Mother Nature. We retreated from aspirations of better care, hospitality, and quality of life in our communities and facilities toward the singular focus of keeping folks safe, alive, and not infected. In short, it felt as if the weight of that pandemic pushed all the progress (albeit not perfected) we had made in the assisted living era back into the nursing home era and made us, once again, old folks' homes.

As an industry, occupancies retreated, too, from averages in the high 80 percent to the low 70 percent range. That number in and of itself tells the story: How, at a time when the number of older adults who need service has never been higher, could occupancies in facilities be lower? The "don't put me in an old folks' home" mentality is alive and well. Like the times when nursing homes were the only game in town, COVID-19 caused us to retreat from the aspirational promise of assisted and independent living—homelike places—to the "safety" mentality of the past; for a moment of time, we went backward.

Before COVID-19, The Springs Living enjoyed 95 percent occupancy on average, a normal investment-grade occupancy rate. But when COVID-19 hit, we had to lock things down, and we threw out the gains we had made in quality of life in order to once again, as an industry, keep residents safe as our primary goal. Keeping people safe is important, but sometimes doing so does not feel very good for the ones being kept safe. In the early stages, keeping people safe was appreciated, but after the vaccine, they wanted their lives back. Safety is important to everyone until it is overpowered by the desire for the dignity of basic personal freedom.

As in every failure, seeds of a greater opportunity have to start somewhere: COVID-19 paved the way to a bright future by deconstructing the ruts of our previous pathways. What is amazing is the timing. The saying "timing is everything" is correct, and it does not go unnoticed that the timing of COVID-19 coincides with the entrance of the greatest opportunity our profession has ever seen—the entrance of the baby boomers into the senior housing and care demographic.

The Big Boom Era

What Kramer called out as the postpandemic/boomer era, I call the big boom era, because it started like the big bang theory, all at once. Two forces collided—the explosion of COVID-19 and the first baby boomers' coming of age and entering the demographic that need support in their lives because of aging. Boomers saw that they would not live locked down for very long, even in the face of a virus that could kill them. They know they aren't getting out of this life alive, and they feel the ticking of the clock. They want to live their life.

For years, prognosticators have been saying that we had better change for the boomers. This is the generation that changed society itself, and it is the generation that will not put up with life in an old folks' home of the 1970s nor, given the choice, will they move into the assisted living buildings of the 2000s without change. The momentum of these two forces of nature, COVID-19 and the baby boomers, will propel the reinvention of an entire industry.

As both COVID-19 and the boomers have blown up the long-term care of the past, what we did in the past is a historical guidepost to be used to navigate the future. As I write this book in the fall of 2023, our industry is in crisis. Occupancies have not fully recovered, nor have margins, and interest rates increased substantially, to the point of putting many operations at risk of loss—operating losses that if companies were forced to sell today would wipe out much of their value. Unless we pivot our organizations to meet the demands of the future and understand what our new customers want, our own organizations may experience a big boom—an explosion that they might not survive. However, the wave of population on the horizon will soon fill even the most challenging communities simply because there are more people with needs than there are physical places for them to live.[3] But filling buildings with bodies should not

---

3   Dana Powell, "Nearly 1 Million New Senior Living Units Needed by 2040," Senior Housing News, October 7, 2019, https://seniorhousingnews.com/2019/10/07/nearly-1-million-new-senior-living-units-needed-by-2040/.

be the standard, because that is what started this whole old folks' problem to start with.

So, where do we go from here? Is there a way to create a time, a place, and an experience that people can look forward to? The senior living experience has been missing some important elements: the focus on quality that leads to comfort, curiosity, and delight. I am offering that the positive natural charge we are looking for is found in the environment and resources we create to support older adults. The main ingredient: people. If you are reading this book, it is highly possible that you are the positive element that can make a difference. The positive charge is found when we fulfill our promises. Quality happens with positive people and places that create an environment that grows relationships even as our bodies are in decline. *The soul and spirit never get old.*

Have you ever read a book that pulled you in and kept you engaged until the last chapter, when the author blows the ending and you sit back in your chair with an "ugh" instead of wanting to read the sequel? No matter how good someone's life was, if the chapters near the end conclude poorly, it can create a generational stigma and hurt. Our profession of long-term care and senior housing and care are eternally important to every older adult and all their family. As professionals in this industry, we must be relentless at getting this right. Our focus must be on the outcome of each person who lives with us or whom we support in their own home. Our resources, our energy, and our focus must be on the quality of each life. To let one person or family we support fall through the cracks is not acceptable. While accomplishing this seems an impossible promise, it is not—it is a positive promise, an aspirational promise and the basis for all cultures of promise, and that's why we must keep making promises.

KEY TAKEAWAYS:

- As Keren Brown observed, what we want for others (safety) is not always what we want for ourselves (autonomy) as we age. The industry needs to balance both.

- COVID-19 and the aging baby boomer generation colliding is forcing reinvention of the industry. Boomers will demand more than what existing models offer.

- Occupancy rates dropped during COVID but are expected to surge as more boomers age into senior housing. However, simply filling buildings should not be the goal—quality of life and experience must improve.

- Key ingredients missing in the past were comfort, curiosity, and delight. The industry needs to create positive environments and experiences people look forward to, not dread.

- The soul and spirit never get old. If the industry can enable more social connections and personal growth in later life stages, demand should increase.

CHAPTER 3

A Different Kind of Promise

Don't implement promises but keep them.

—C. S. Lewis

The new kind of promise I am talking about is an aspirational promise. Promises come in different sizes and shapes. Solemn promises, legal promises, political promises, marketing promises, and fairy-tale promises are all defined and well known. Aspirational promises are also a type of promise; they are a mixture of solemn and fairy-tale promises and are expressed as a verb. An aspirational promise is also unconditional. Aspirational promises are not a guarantee of perfection but an unconditional commitment to work toward an outcome. I am not talking about a promise to simply try. To simply try, make an attempt—this is an action based on limited attempts or a time duration that checks the "I tried" box. The difference in an unconditional promise is that it is infinite effort backed by values, belief, and determination. Like Winston Churchill said when Britain seemed lost to Germany in World War II, "Never, never, never give up." An aspirational promise is like a turbocharger on a car that changes the normal environment and gives you that extra power you need. Like you can feel the turbocharged power, you can feel the genuine commitment and determination of an aspirational promise.

When I made my first promise to my grandma, I didn't fully understand there was seemingly no possible way it could be kept. How could I understand? I was just a kid who adored his grandmother. Yet I made it with all the emotion and determination of someone who knew they could keep it. Folks expect most promises to be kept, but few believe an aspirational promise will be kept. As innocent children, we mean our promises; we cross our hearts and hope to die not knowing how or if we will have the ability to keep them in the future.

If you look closely enough, every worthy human endeavor starts with a promise. Every promise of love, and even dark promises of revenge. Promises are made to yourself, your family, or some idea or cause. Every successful company or organization starts with a promise. Companies write a mission statement, which is an implicit indication that the founders are making a promise to their customers, employees, and themselves to do better, to do bigger, or to make a difference. The promise I made to my grandmother was powerful, like a seed. It seemed small at the time. But like a seed, it carried the potential to grow beyond my wildest imagination.

Nature holds many clues to life. An ancient parable speaks of the tiny mustard seed growing into a large, sturdy plant and becoming the greatest of all trees. Nature has rules, and as much as we think we can circumvent or overpower them, we cannot. What we can do is nurture our promises with emotion, intelligence, commitment, and hard work, hoping that they will in time grow. That is the power of a small promise planted deep in your heart and properly cared for. When you understand the power of a promise, you can not only achieve personal success but do it in a manner that makes a difference and leaves the world a better place. Just like in nature, not every seed grows to full fruition, but unless we start with the promise, we are guaranteed not to see our dreams grow. Hopefully along the way we don't choose to uproot or fail to water a promise—a sure way to never see a result. That fateful trip to the nursing home would turn into my life's work because it planted a seed that would lie dormant for over twenty years before it began to grow. Yet the hope of the promise made remained like a cherished fairy tale in my mind and heart, and I never forgot the day I made that promise.

I think I already understood, in the character of my grandmother, that promises should be sacred. When we were kids, we would "pinky promise" our friends, and many of us were taught by our moms, dads, grandparents, or other adult mentors to keep our promises. At some point, for some of us earlier than others, our childhoods collided with the real world, and we learned that not many people actually keep their promises. After all, pinky promises are made by children, and no one expects them to be an enforceable contract. But they are our first brush with the concept of a promise. Even as children, when someone broke their promise, it was grounds for not being recess friends. Somehow those early experiences serve to inform our point of view and piece together our human development puzzle. When we know someone will keep their promise, we trust. But it seems rare that promises are kept, leading us to avoid making and believing in promises.

Keeping promises is so important and ingrained into our social and economic reality that to be labeled a promise breaker is the kiss of death for relationships, both personal and business. Breaking a promise to yourself can lead to lower self-esteem and lack of confidence. (Think of a time when you promised yourself you would exercise more in order to be healthy—and two weeks later, your running shoes were still hidden in the back of your closet.)

For businesses, when public companies do not hit their earnings targets, their stock price declines. When they overpromise and underdeliver to customers, their reputation declines and they will lose business, and if a persistent gap between promises to their customers and what they deliver continues, they may lose their entire business.

It's Hard to Keep a Promise

It's hard to keep a promise. As adults, when people let us down and we let others down, we become cynical and weary with our newfound knowledge of the fallibility of promises. People break their promises for many reasons, most of which are not because they are evil or dishonest. Many break their promises because, at the time, they don't realize that what they are promising is impossible to keep. We have too little information. Many people pleasers have good intentions when they make promises, not realizing the impossibility of their vows.

Through experience we learn that many companies that promise to help us lose weight, feel younger, or even grow our hair back don't live up to their promises. As consumers we become skeptical of the "tin men" of industry, realizing that they have been trained in techniques to prod or entice us to part with our hard-earned treasure in trade for some manufactured trinket—a handful of beads or a necklace of wampum. Whole enterprises have been created to help you keep your promises and guide you toward achievement and happiness. To say "I promise" in today's business world is to gain looks of distrust and skepticism, yet fulfilling our promises is at the heart of success in business.

The smart play for business is to not make promises that have less than a 100 percent chance of success, but then neither would they grow and expand. As those of us with decades of experience know, the only thing that is actually expected is the unexpected. Aspirational promises give us permission to pivot, fix problems, and overcome the inevitable difficulties because rarely do opportunities with guaranteed success come along; if we waited for certainty, we would never progress, innovate, or change the world for the better.

My promise to Grandma was an aspirational promise—a different type of promise, the type that is needed to make change. It was aspirational and had little chance of success at the time it was made. This type of promise is made to be broken (not intentionally) because it is evolutionary and therefore will fail before it ever succeeds. An aspirational promise is the type of promise that rallies generations and coalesces entrepreneurs with capital and people to advance behind a common vision and mission. An aspirational promise is the promise I made to my grandmother and one that our industry needs to realize we have made to each person who lives in our communities as well as their family.

Promise Culture Promises

Cultures of promise make two kinds of promises: aspirational promises and business promises. Understanding the distinction between the two is perhaps the number one role of a leader in a culture of promise. Aspirational promises are made with the knowledge that they will be broken because they encompass the powerful, big ideas and mission of a vision; business promises must not be broken. Both are equally important to your reputation. Your reputation and credibility are everything in business and, I would contend, in life. Business promises are the ones you make to any stakeholder that has a deadline or definite measurable outcome (or KPI). For example, a business promise to a customer could be to make sure their billing is done accurately and on time. It could be that you will provide a specific service that you agreed to or that you will solve a problem within a particular time frame. To an employee, a business promise is that you will pay them on time, follow your employee handbook, or send them to training. To an investor, it could be that you will have an investment report to them on a certain date or that you will send them a check by a certain date. A vendor is owed a business promise to pay our bills on time. Anyone who is a stakeholder in your organization can be owed a business promise. Ignore this fact at your own peril.

A manager at one of our communities years ago neglected to promptly approve our invoices to a certain vendor. Innocently, he felt he was doing our company a favor by helping us manage cash flow and sticking it to the vendor. It turns out this had been a common practice at the organization he had previously worked for. In his mind, he was making a shrewd business decision. The problem was twofold. First, our contract required us to pay current invoices every thirty days. Since he didn't have the contract, he was unaware of our promise in writing, which was a business promise. Second, the vendor's family had lived in the community and knew a lot of people. His mother belonged to the local country club and senior center. When she learned we didn't pay our bills, she made it her personal mission to tell all her friends. How could we expect our customers to pay on time when we didn't pay on time? Our reputation took a hit.

The Power of the Aspirational Promise

The promise I made that day to my grandmother was a different kind of promise: it was an aspirational promise. Aspirational promises can be the most powerful promises if they come from a deep belief or emotional commitment. Aspirational promises mean as much, if not more, to the maker, the promisor, as to the one who was promised. They connect the promisor in a deeply emotional way to the fulfillment of the promise. It's a promise that "I will take care of you." An aspirational promise carries with it a positive charge that is magnetic when focused on fixing a problem.

Every successful company or organization started with an aspirational promise, whether or not they realized it or thought of it in this way. Think of the old Burger King tagline, "Have it your way," or Disneyland's promise that it was "the Happiest Place on Earth." BMW created a culture where every employee works to create "the ultimate driving machine."

Sure, these taglines and slogans are meant to convey to the customer what a company does. But in the very best organizations, they are more than that. They are the promise of that organization to their customer, and that promise is powerful. Knowing your promise gets to the root of your purpose for existing, and unless you have intense clarity around that, your organization will never truly be great. Michael Gerber said in his book *The eMyth: Why Most Businesses Don't Work and What to Do About It*, "Clarity is king." When you, your employees, and your customers know essentially why you exist, you unleash your full potential.

Like unconditional love, these promises don't end when faced with failure or reality or deadlines. They reveal an opportunity to fill an unmet need. No guarantee of fulfillment exists for aspirational promises. An aspirational promise is about not giving up. They require grit and tenacity and are anchored in your beliefs and values; love and passion fuel aspirational promises.

> *Aspirational promises can seem impossible ... while the odds may be against you, it does not mean, even if you end in failure, that you have failed. You only fail if you stop.*

Aspirational promises often seem impossible to everyone but to the promise maker. Most if not all your closest advisors will consider you not serious and doubt your ability to achieve success. While the odds may be against you, it does not mean, even if you end in failure, that you have failed. You only fail if you stop. That failure can be used as fertilizer to grow the seed. Aspirational promises are powerful but carry risks and have to be mixed with a focused goal, preparation, strategy, hard work, and, of course, a lot of luck. Luck seems to show up the harder we work.

An aspirational promise cannot bloom just because you want it to. (If only that were so!) Just as in nature, getting fruit off a tree takes time. Patience and persistence are key ingredients. The saying "timing is everything" is a good example of waiting for the right time by being patient. The waiting can produce risk and uncertainty, but so can moving too quickly. No venture is guaranteed success, and understanding how timing impacts success comes only through experience. The basketball coach John Wooden taught his players to "be quick, but don't hurry." In the business of taking care of others, you are growing relationships, and that takes time. I would expand on the great quote by saying, "Don't try to force or hurry a relationship, but be quick to solve its problems."

Aspirational promises are directional and hold the power to capture our time and attention and motivate us because they connect to our gut, our intuition, our heart, and our passion. That passion produces energy, and that energy attracts collaboration, innovation, and momentum with magnetic force. The deeper the conviction, the deeper the commitment. It pulls together like-minded individuals into a synergy by creating clarity that, when mixed with capacity and experience, turns ideas into reality.

The promise I made to my grandmother was not thought through thoroughly at the time it was made. Instead, it was emotional and instantaneous. Not much thought was initially involved, just heart, and it would take decades to put the thinking parts together. Saying yes seemed like the only course of action. I am sure she never expected me to keep it, nor in all likelihood did she think I could. I know for a fact that I was not sure, either, that I could or would keep it, but that promise held some dormant power that would guide my decisions and the way I evaluated the course of my life and career.

My aspirational promise acted like a magnetic attractor while also filtering opportunities in my life. It was a connector for people, capital, and opportunity. The promise prioritized, highlighted, and attracted opportunities that would push me closer to its fulfillment. That promise and the emotion behind it had some unseen magnetic force. Unbeknownst to me, through the years it would nudge me, helping me gather the pieces of my puzzle. Those pieces came in the form of jobs I took, people I met, and skills I learned, like gathering hidden badges in a video game.

In a culture of promise, we must fulfill two distinct and different promises to all the stakeholders. The power of aspirational promises is the heart and soul of a culture of promise, but they are not enough to make an organization successful. To be truly successful, an organization must also fulfill its business promises to its stakeholders, which includes its customers, employees, vendors, and investors. Yet in a culture of promise, you cannot succeed in fulfilling your business promises without a true commitment to your aspirational promise. Let me explain.

Both promises require the other; they are not mutually exclusive. They are like two sides of a coin. Business promises without the full commitment to your aspirational promise will feel cold and robotic to the customer and your employees. Aspirational promises without the ability to fulfill your business promises will doom the organization to mediocrity and limit its ability to grow in a meaningful way. While this seems obvious and simple, it is not. I am proposing that unless you combine a full commitment to both promises, you will not achieve the full potential in your endeavors, especially ones that promise to care for others.

Aspirational promises give life and meaning to our business promises. The value of an aspirational promise is the hope it gives and the permission to fail until you get it right. This point of view is critical in a culture of promise. Why? Because it normalizes the day-to-day fear of failing at our promises and lets us mentally and emotionally push through the difficulties and failures. When day after day we show up to work only to confront the problems of our customers—in our profession it's a family member or resident—the burden can be heavy. That burden, unless lightened, is perhaps the number one contributor to turnover in senior housing and care. Maintaining a culture of promise helps us retain our energy and commitment.

I recently heard of a chef who quit the senior housing industry because he could not handle the constant criticism of his food. In a culture of promise, you understand it's not about the food. It's about that person being relevant and valued for their contribution, a human need that feeds the spirit like food feeds the body. You must encourage and hear criticism to know that you are being effective. If you do not encourage feedback and deal with it well, you will train your customers that it's a waste of time to talk to you, and that translates to you not caring for them. Stifling criticism might bring you temporary relief, but it will not stop it. Your unsatisfied customers will simply turn their backs to you and tell the outside world, and when that happens, it is the beginning of the end. Ignoring even the smallest complaint is to start down the road of becoming an old folks' home. Instead, you must create a culture that normalizes feedback, encourages feedback, and treats each one with significance. Don't just check the box on this; believe in it and live it, and you will attract success like a flower does a bee. If you take anything away from this book, take this point: *problems are our greatest opportunity.*

> *Cultures of Promise embrace problems as fuel for success. Problems are why we are in business.*

If people didn't have problems to solve, they would not need you and you would not be in business. People come to Cultures of Promise for the exact reason they have problems. Expecting their problems to magically go away is insanity; it is not going to happen. Their problems should diminish because of the services and support our organizations offer, but they will never go away. Instead of expecting problems to go away, look at the type of problems. Let's be honest—many people like to complain. They complain about their bursitis, their pacemaker, or even their grandchildren. Complaints are just a way that folks engage with other folks. I am not condoning this method of human interaction because it would be much easier if everyone was an optimist, but they are not. Simply recognizing this can take a heavy weight off your shoulders.

Culture of promise organizations need to change the paradigm on problems. Embrace them; get excited about them; run toward them—not away. Incentivize your employees to find them and solve them. Turn it into a quest, a game ... or offer a bonus structure. Your ultimate success will not be in the elimination of problems but in understanding their severity. Since you will never eliminate complaints, judge your success on the type of complaint. A complaint that one of your residents has not been given their medication on time is not the kind you want to routinely see; if you do, you have a serious issue that needs to be confronted. But a complaint that "the carrots are not cooked the way I did it at home" tells you that person is engaged and offering a suggestion. Do not take offense from the complaint; treat it with legitimacy and offer to elevate it, because the promise to fix it is an aspirational promise.

Aspirational promises are messy and sometimes hard to understand and can even mean different things for different people. Aspirational promises are made in organizational cultures that promise something personal, subjective, and not always defined the same way by each customer, like the promise to "take care of you" found in organizations like senior living, day care, or a nonprofit endeavor. Because they are designed for that type of organization, they require the promisor to use judgment based on values. This is the messy part, and this is where these organizations must have people with high emotional quotients (EQs) guiding customer relationship decisions. The emotional quotient overrides what IQ says you should do for the income statement at that point of time. Yet when you make decisions with EQ and IQ, you succeed at a deeper and longer-lasting level.

Let me explain. At one of our communities recently, we had an independent living resident who needed more assistance and support to move to the assisted living portion of our community. Emotional and coming to grips with the aging process and the stage of life they were in, this gentleman was upset that the toilet in his new assisted living apartment was at a different height from the floor than the one in his independent apartment, which he was used to. The problem is that it wasn't. The new apartment's toilet seat was at the same height. Reasoning and showing him the tape measurement was not working because of the challenges he was going through and their impact on his mental capacity. Besides, it wasn't about the toilet seat; it was about his diminishing ability to control his life. Our business promises to his family did not require us to replace the toilet seat, but our aspirational promise did.

Our customer relations manager, Greg, made a quick trip to Home Depot and, upon returning, pulled the new toilet seat out of the box and replaced the seat, achieving satisfaction from our customer even though the height remained the same.

That is what I mean by messy. You cannot write a policy that covers all these situations other than empowering people to use judgment to solve problems, rarely two that are alike. Greg had the authority and EQ to solve that, and he also had the IQ to realize that solving this problem, even though we were not required to, was the smart thing. It was the smart thing because that story has spread to other families and customers and builds our reputation for quality. The smart pay was the relationship and reputational payoff; besides, it was the right thing to do. That is what I mean when I say aspirational promises can be messy!

I understand that not all the complaints are even real or legitimate, but that is not the point. Even if you are right, you will be wrong if you do not take every complaint with sincere intent to understand its origin. However, I am not saying you should let people game you or take advantage of you. You'll know the difference when you see it.

Likewise, an industry that made its first attempt at caring for older adults in the 1960s and 1970s made a similar aspirational promise. One that promised to try. I am sure some smart people believed their policy ideas would result in happiness ever after. It did not. Yet an aspirational promise never gives up. When it falls short, it doubles down and pivots just like each person, each organization, and our policymakers must do.

What Powers an Aspirational Promise?

What powers your ability to make aspirational promises comes from deep inside; it's your values, a wrong you see that needs righting, a meaningful experience that needs propagating, or an opportunity to change the world for the better. What gives us the power to never give up is that an aspirational promise is completely tied to our why. Our "why" is the personal reason we make the impossible promise, and it is the magnetic attraction that will coalesce others to join the mission by connecting with our purpose. Our why is our source. Based on more than emotion, our why connects to our beliefs and the deep parts of us that fulfill or help us seek our purpose in life. External successes, while nice, can never match the satisfaction of a life well-lived in pursuit of purpose. Our purpose is not about easy or neat or simple but about that deep knowing of satisfaction that in the point that we are alive, in the place we are alive, and based on the connection of events in our lives, we are pursuing better. Knowing ourselves and being a part of something bigger than our individual lives, a connectedness to something good produces the ability to get back up after being knocked down. It gives us the inspiration to try again, even when we are physically and mentally exhausted.

> *He who has a why to live for can bear almost any how.*
> *—Nietzsche*

Knowing your why is the start of our journey. Your future why is linked to your past and your story. The right answer is always a connection of events, even if the past events of your life cause you to go in a completely new direction. And my why, my connection of events, came from a source called Lehman Hot Springs.

KEY TAKEAWAYS:

- An "aspirational promise" is different than a typical promise–it is a commitment to continuous improvement driven by core values and beliefs rather than just trying to achieve a specific end goal. The senior living industry needs more of this aspirational mindset.

- Senior living organizations must fulfill two types of promises: aspirational promises tied to their mission and values, and business promises made to stakeholders like residents, employees, and investors. All are critical.

- When addressing complaints, emotional intelligence and empathy (EQ)for residents must override strict business logic (IQ) at times.

- The quality of human relationships, not just quality standards or metrics, defines the quality of life for residents. Enabling meaningful connections and purpose should be the priority.

- Turnover in the industry is often high because the burden of unmet expectations and problems feels too heavy over time without the context of a higher aspirational purpose.

- Solving problems is our greatest opportunity. If people didn't have problems, we wouldn't have a reason to exist.

- Run towards problems, not away from them.

CHAPTER 4

The Source of a Promise

Integrity is conforming reality to our words—in other words, keeping promises and fulfilling expectations.

–Stephen Covey

It was 1996, and at thirty-one years old, I had just started my own company to develop and acquire apartment buildings. Balancing life with a young family and new business, I always made time to mow Grandma Lillian's lawn. I was living on SW Fifth Avenue in Portland, Oregon, a city that was thriving, clean, and safe, when a brochure arrived in the mail. The National Multifamily Housing Council, which I liked to attend from time to time, was to be held in Atlanta, Georgia. But this year, I noticed a preconference session on senior housing. I had never seen an offering for a senior housing conference before. Emerson said in his essay "Self-Reliance," "A man should learn to detect and watch that gleam of light which flashes across his mind from within …" The flyer caught my eye.

The conference was in late May, just before the annual trip we took to visit my wife Julie's family on a South Carolina beach. I decided to head to Atlanta early, attend the seminar, and then meet Julie for the family reunion. *That decision changed my life and caused my new company to pivot even as it was just getting started.*

The session was held in one of the small breakout rooms at the Atlanta Convention Center. I walked in and took a seat on the left side toward the back. Tom Clark was in charge of the senior housing efforts of the council, and he was just introducing the feature speaker, Tracy Lux. Tracy, a dynamic speaker and knowledgeable marketing expert in the area of senior housing, was a pioneer in the industry. I am not sure any of us knew it at the time, but this session and its few dozen participants were laying the groundwork for an entire industry that was just emerging out of infancy. As Tracy and Tom and market research specialist Evelyn Howard spoke of the demographic waves and the advancements in what was a fairly new concept, assisted living, I was enthralled. Asking questions and scribbling notes, I took it all in. The first day's session concluded, and I made my way to the front of the room to introduce myself to Tom.

I patiently waited my turn as other attendees asked questions or chitchatted about various topics. These moments are always awkward for me, standing in an unorganized queue listening but not really participating. I considered just heading out and trying again the next day, but I persisted. Finally, I introduced myself. Tom was professional through to his core but had a kindness about him I still remember. I awkwardly admitted that I wasn't quite sure why I was there other than I had a grandmother who wanted no part of living in what she considered an old folks' home. The conversation gained momentum and then was interrupted.

"Have you met Tracy?" Tom asked as she approached to tell Tom goodbye.

"I haven't, but I enjoyed your session today," I said, sticking my hand out to offer a greeting and introduction. I mentioned where I was from.

"Oregon?" she said, with a hint of inquisitive excitement. "I think Oregon is at the forefront of innovation in senior housing and skilled nursing care." The room was slowly clearing as attendees made their way to the exit.

"Do you have any dinner plans?" Tom asked me, just as another attendee stepped into the conversation, singling out Tracy with their body language.

I didn't, and he invited me to join him on top of a famous hotel in downtown Atlanta, where the restaurant continually rotated 360 degrees. From that seventy-two-story vantage point, I felt like I could see the future.

I arrived at the restaurant at seven. As we sat down at our table, he said, "Tell me about Oregon." I wanted to be the one asking a lot of questions about senior housing, but he beat me to the punch, intrigued by Tracy's comment about Oregon's innovations in caring for older adults.

I was proud of my pioneer roots. As I rambled, my cocktail loosening my tongue a bit, I told of how our family had come across the Oregon Trail in 1846 and 1886. The latter group, the Stubblefields from Texas, migrated after retreating from West Texas Comanches back into the trees and mountains of Arkansas for a brief period. Seven generations of Oregonians, our family included early settlers who risked the journey for a chance at a good life free of the Civil War aftermath and hostilities of Quanah Parker and associates. Having survived a few encounters with warring Comanche raiding parties, my great-great-grandfather simply wanted a place to raise his family in peace, and Oregon was it. Settlers on the Oregon Trail had a decision to make at Independence Rock. Do they go left, toward California and gold, or stay steady on the main branch of the Oregon Trail? Oregon didn't offer the get-rich-quick allure of California, but it did offer a great place to ranch, farm, and raise a family in relative peace. The Stubblefields were about family and hard work, and so Oregon it was.

Tom was intrigued and probed for more information.

"I was born in Pendleton, Oregon," I continued.

"You mean where Pendleton Wool is from?"

"Exactly," I replied, happy that he had a frame of reference. "But I really grew up at a place called Lehman Hot Springs, just south of Pendleton." Tom wanted to know more.

Pushing my plate of food aside, I grabbed my water glass for a prop, put it directly in front of me, and said, "The whole place is built around the source—natural hot springs." Without a pause, I explained, "Over fifty artesian springs bubble out of the ground and form a hot stream. The water emerges at between 125 and 150 degrees Fahrenheit. It is collected in a series of pools that cover almost nine thousand square feet for soaking and swimming." He could tell I loved the place where I grew up.

From left to right: Fancho Stubblefield Sr.; Fancho Fee Stubblefield Jr. (author); and Fancho Fee Stubblefield Sr. in front of pools circa 1970.

I grabbed the butter dish and placed it close to the glass. "The original lodge was built by James Lehman in the 1880s, but my grandfather tore it down and built a grand lodge in 1933, eight years after he purchased Lehman. Then he built cabins here." I placed a fork sideways along the pool near the lodge to indicate their location. "Then there was a camping ground here," using my knife for that location, "a dance hall here, and eventually RV parking here." Surrounded, the glass with utensils and condiments represented the master plan of the resort like spokes on a wheel with the hot springs as the hub.

"How far is Lehman from the nearest town?" Tom asked.

"Over an hour, depending on which town you are coming from," I answered. "No one would come out to this remote canyon if the hot water wasn't there. That is why Fancho built all the different housing around the springs."

"It must be pretty special water for folks to drive that far, especially at the turn of the century, just to soak in a pool," he stated.

I added, "The water is magical. It's like a fountain of youth. When you soak in it, your aches and pains fade and your skin becomes smooth and soft like when you were young. It's all due to a perfect mineral content that absorbs in trace amounts into your skin as you swim and soak. Traces of minerals like lithium, which is known as a mood stabilizer, help you simply relax. The high silica content makes your skin smooth and soft, and the natural magnesium absorbs through your skin at a pace just right for your body. It is said to improve your circulation and relieve stress, is good for your internal organs, and relaxes the muscles. And if you want the best sleep of your life, soak right before bedtime.

"While my grandfather was a big personality, it was my grandmother that kept the wheels on," I said, remembering. "I spent much of my childhood around her, raking pine needles in the campgrounds, picking up litter, and eating her homemade hamburgers and milkshakes. I remember older folks were always around and soaking in the pools. And with the health benefits, I can now see why. It must have made them feel younger."

"You know," Tom said, pausing thoughtfully. "I think you have just described the perfect metaphor for building senior housing."

I held his gaze for a moment, my mind working to understand his words. "What do you mean?"

It took a few moments for his revelation to sink in, but when it came it was like the sky parting for me. Tom was connecting the dots: it gave me great clarity, and I could see the future. He explained first that as the director and visionary for senior housing for the National Association of Home Builders Multifamily Housing Council, he had visited many retirement communities and assisted living and skilled nursing facilities. I was beginning to see that Tom was very conceptual, a thinker before his time, and he was just about to give me a glimpse of his years of knowledge in one simple story.

He explained, "Lehman Hot Springs offers, in my experience, a model of how we should look at senior housing development and operations. You just told me that no one would likely go to the remote canyon where Lehman is located if the hot springs weren't there, right?"

"Yes," I said slowly, wondering where he was going with this.

"Well, if you ask me, folks don't want to go to senior housing just for the location or the real estate, but they will go there because of the care and compassion of the people who work there." I could tell his excitement was building.

"In my opinion, the healing hot water is analogous to the care and compassion of the people who staff the communities." He pointed at my water glass representing the hot springs. "Imagine that water glass without any water. Would anyone pick it up to take a drink?" He shook his head. "No one wants to come to a building just for a building; they come for the care—they come for the way you make them feel and how you support their lives. The most important thing we do in senior housing is not building buildings but caring!"

I let the concept sink in. The power of this idea, in this moment, sent my mind searching, remembering, and trying to connect it to a clear path forward. I knew this was one of those rare times in life when you hear a life-changing thought. I just wasn't sure what it meant. We teased the concept further by hitting the verbal tennis ball back and forth. The warm water represented the care we gave: warm, healing, and comforting. But we also realized that giving that care can only be done by people who genuinely cared and could provide love, support, and comfort. Just like the unique and authentic minerals of the hot springs, our communities must have people with authentic values. Their values needed to align with complete dedication to the care and service of the people who lived in our communities.

No flashing lights or directional signs marked the way forward. I had the sense that this seemingly random trip to go to a random seminar and random dinner was not random at all. I never set out to be in senior housing. Hell, I didn't even know it was a thing or could be a career. As the hours after our dinner ticked past, I felt the moment fading into some cabinet in my head, filed away for another time. I was not fully unaware that I had just gathered a piece of an ancient medallion like in the Indiana Jones movies, except unlike Harrison Ford, I had no idea what I had just found. This was two years before I would build our first community and many years before I would get the full picture of the metaphor and realize the power of the story of Lehman Hot Springs, Lax-ayxpa. A unique and sacred place and a deep love for my grandmother were the sources for my aspirational promise to her and an industry.

Ester Short, my maternal grandmother, on left holding ribbon; Lillian Stubblefield on right. Fee Stubblefield getting ready to cut the ribbon at Lancaster Woods, today called The Springs at Willowcreek.

Sure enough, my grandmother cut the ribbon for our first community in Salem, Oregon (at the time, we called it Lancaster Woods). It was seventy-six units of residential care and assisted living spread out on a three-acre campus and designed as large one-story homes. Grandma was not a social butterfly, and I wanted to build something homelike, warm, and comfortable. After all, I had made an aspirational promise that she could stay in her own home, and since staying in her own home was not achievable anymore, my aspirational promise led me to build this community that was designed to look and feel like her home. I will never forget the grand opening in 1998. It was the proudest day of my professional career to have there both of my maternal grandmothers, Lillian Stubblefield and Ester Short.

She had already turned the shovel at the groundbreaking ceremony and knew what I was up to.

This time I was driving as we approached the community more than twenty years after my first trip with her to that nursing home. We parked and walked into the first building. A long time had passed since we'd last entered a senior building together, and this time it wasn't a nursing home. Gone were the long hallways filled with fluorescent light. Gone was the front desk that felt like a guard station. What she did see was a homelike living room bathed in light and warmth provided by the design and the hearts and smiles of the people who worked there.

As we stood just inside the door and she took in the surroundings, she looked at me, smiled, and said, "This feels just like home." My heart soared—*mission accomplished.* I thought, *She loves the place.* My mind raced ahead to which apartment I would show her, hoping she would like the actual apartments. To my surprise, her next statement set me on my heels. "This will be really nice for those old people."

"What?" My mind tried to process her statement. "Those old people?" I said, questioning. "Grandma, you are ninety!"

CHAPTER 5

A Promise Is Not Enough

I promise. And when I promise something, I never ever break that promise. Ever!

—Rapunzel, *Tangled*

It wasn't until my grandma had her second heart attack that she moved into The Springs at Clackamas Woods Assisted Living. A stubborn pioneer, I envied her tenacity and toughness, but congenital heart disease caused cognitive dementia, and her ability to make any rational decision except for the ability to always say no had left her skill set years before. Our second community, The Springs at Clackamas Woods in Milwaukie, Oregon, was closer to her home and doctors. It opened shortly after the first one had become successful. That first community had filled to capacity in a short time even without her moving in.

Her doctor was clear and told us in no uncertain terms that she could not stay in her own home any longer without full-time care, which our family combined could not afford. The years of us piecing together support for her had proven frustrating and an impossible task considering that she never wanted to bother us or keep us from living our lives. She needed help but refused to ask for it, and her living conditions deteriorated. With us all busy with kids, jobs, and careers, the task had mainly fallen to my aunt, mom, and dad, but I still mowed her lawn.

The night we moved her personal belongings in, my cousin David and I drove toward her house in his Ford F-250 pickup, heading to her future. A firefighter, David was used to rescuing people. His mom had packed most of what Grandma would be taking to her one-bedroom assisted living apartment at The Springs in Clackamas. She was to be discharged from the hospital the next day; she was ninety-two.

I didn't know if she felt I had fulfilled my promise to her by enabling her to stay in her home until age ninety-two or if I and our family had failed her by moving her into a community. I did know that my promise to her had been the spark for a company that was growing and innovating and working every day to pull people's experiences away from the nursing home inertia of old folks' homes and the stigma of a poor quality of life. For me, that moment was an unusual mix of loss and pride, but for her it was just a sense of loss, even though she was moving to a community that she had inspired. I have learned that any change, even good change, is accompanied by a sense of loss.

Her first few days in her new apartment were a struggle. Her deep bias against anything that was not a single-family home with a yard was strong. But I understood the source of her distrust. I also could see that for anyone moving out of their home, their castle, their dream, it didn't really matter how nice the building was or how kind the people who worked there were. It's a point in your life that seems like it will never arrive, and then all of a sudden, it does. Life is full of many milestones.

Remember when you got your driver's license? Moved out of the house or went off to college? The excitement and sense of adventure and the feeling of hope and invincibility, even if we were a little scared and unsure. Now imagine it's taken away—your world seems smaller, less hopeful, like when you can feel just a few pages left in your right hand nearing the end of a good book. Our single-family home and our automobiles are cultural cornerstones and define the American dream. Losing both can be devastating.

Maslow Explains

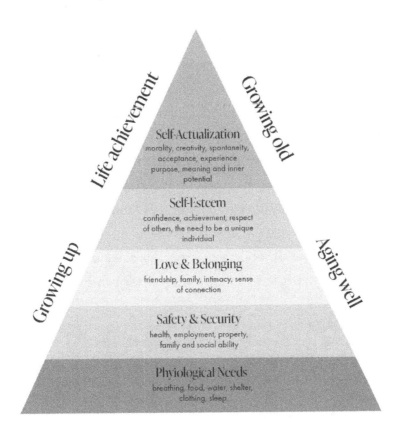

Maslow's hierarchy of needs tells the story.[4] The Maslow pyramid consists of five levels of human need as the mountain in life we climb. As children, we start the climb up one side of the mountain with the support of family or institutions. At first, our parents or support structure provide the basics of need: physiological needs like food and clothing. They keep us safe in the next level of safety. Then, as we gain independence and move out of the house, we get education and jobs so we can assume the climb under our own power. We ascend past love and belonging as we gain friendships and committed relationships to help carry the load or raise a family of our own. Our youthful energy defies gravity as we climb higher (see Figure on page 57). Through trial and error, good times and bad, we hit the self-esteem and social levels as we build confidence, achievement, and relationships and become a unique individual with independence and choice. All this leads us toward Maslow's pinnacle of life, self-actualization.

Hopefully you are on your way toward that point or have already achieved it. You may define it as you choose, potentially with careers, a dream house, children, grandchildren, or personal accomplishments. While each of us gets to create our own self-actualizing recipe, the one ingredient that it must contain is relationships. The quality of our relationships defines the quality of our lives. (See the TED Talk of Robert Waldinger, the director of Harvard's Study of Adult Development, one of the world's longest studies of adult life.[5]) And if we are lucky, some of our other dreams may even come true. But dreams when you are young look different from when you are on the other

---

4   Abraham H. Maslow, "A Theory of Human Motivation," Simply Psychology, accessed June 23, 2023, https://www.simplypsychology.org/maslow.html.

5   Robert J. Waldinger, "What Makes a Good Life? Lessons from the Longest Study on Happiness," Harvard Gazette, April 11, 2017, https://news.harvard.edu/gazette/story/2017/04/over-nearly-80-years-harvard-study-has-been-showing-how-to-live-a-healthy-and-happy-life/.

side of fifty years old. Next thing you know, we are sixty, seventy, and eighty and saying what my grandma always said: "Oh brother, where did the time go?"

In time, and because of that passage of time and gravity, life changes. Those forces eventually keep us from reaching the sun, and the weight of them slowly pushes us down the other side of Maslow's pyramid. Soon, those lofty goals and dreams of self-actualization aren't quite as important. Further descending, self-esteem takes some hits next as our bodies sag and break down, and we have to come to grips with the fact that we don't look the same in the mirror as we feel inside. Then the reality of time comes for our friends and those we love, pushing us further toward the future awaiting us.

Then the moment arrives when half of us realize we are not safe or secure in our own home, or for the other half of us who are deniers, our kids come home for a holiday to find us with nothing but ice cream and toast in the refrigerator and empty bottles of our prescriptions that have not been refilled. Even more of us are awakened to reality by the bright lights of the ER as our family or friends stand around the bed and we hear the doctor say something like "Lillian, you cannot stay in your home alone anymore."

I witnessed that moment for my grandmother and saw the sense of loss in her eyes. She had fallen all the way down Maslow's pyramid to be rescued by strangers in uniforms and told that she had to give up her seemingly last grasp on her perceived independence. As a family we had done our best to hold the line against the weight of time, all the while putting strain on our own lives, which made her feel like she was a bother. She didn't want to be a burden.

As she listened to the doctor patronizingly congratulate her for living alone until age ninety-two, I can imagine what was going through her head. I can promise you it was that she did not *feel* ninety-two years old. Her inner age was likely younger.

When she was sixty-four, my grandpa Fancho died, and then she was free from caring for a spouse who'd had a stroke and free of serving the public at Lehman Hot Springs. Perhaps that was her inner age? For some of us it's older than our chronological age, but for most, it's younger, perhaps by ten years or more. Even though she understood that I had built the company to improve what I saw lacking in an industry and to fulfill a promise to her specifically, she felt a sense of resigned loss and grief, and I felt guilt.

Even today I wrestle with the notion that I let her down, unsure if I fulfilled the promise. For her, moving into The Springs at Clackamas Woods was the realization that time had caught up to her, and unlike our escape from the nursing home so many years before, there was no way to escape the reality that time comes for us all.

Yet while the move out of her single-family home and into her multifamily home was perceived as loss of independence, she actually began to realize it also set her free. Gone were her feelings of being a burden by relying on the family. She no longer had use for the apologies about taking time out of her children's and grandchildren's lives. While she teased us about being "put" in there, she knew we loved her and was thankful. She learned that the support we offered in the community was not unlike the support she got from hearing aids and a walker. Now she had real-life humans who supported her life, which gave her independence from being a burden, and that she liked.

Perseverance and Aspirational Failures

You might expect me to tell you how great life for my grandma was living in the community that she'd inspired. I owned the community and was committed to it being the best quality. But the reality was it did not go great. We could never get the food good enough, some of her neighbors annoyed her, and our housekeepers did not clean to her standards. I constantly heard, "When can I go home?" We had built a great homelike environment, and in her apartment she was surrounded by things she loved, like her old patterned rug, which now covers the floor of my office, her beloved TV, art, and, yes, that dark-green, floral-patterned recliner. More importantly, the community was filled with kind and generous people who served her and loved her and no long linoleum halls or buzzing fluorescent lights. She had her own bed, not a hospital bed with rails, and a freezer full of ice cream. No doubt we had made life better compared to her friend's nursing home so long ago in Mission, Oregon. But in the end, I felt like I failed not only her but myself.

My grandma lived at The Springs at Clackamas Woods until she was ninety-six, and on June 20, 2004, she passed away alone, in the night, the way she would have wanted. As I reflect on those years, I am haunted by the things we could have done better. We failed too many times to make sure the food was good, we failed to staff all the shifts with people who were excellent at their jobs, we failed to perform, on more than one occasion, all the tasks on her care plan, and the final failure was one I will never forget.

The night she passed, our team neglected to call me, and I found out about the greatest loss in my life from a third party in the middle of the night! As a family member who already felt guilt that their loved one was living somewhere they didn't want to be, how could my own company make this mistake? How could I learn from someone outside my own company that she had died? I was angry and hurt. We were a small company, and I knew every employee by name. In the end, it didn't even matter that I owned the company and started it for her. Not finding out from our team still bothers me. That was the moment I realized that not only are our residents our customers, but their families are too. The way we prepare for and handle transitions when a resident passes can make a generational impact. Every individual and family have things that are eternally important at these important moments. The world changes when someone we love leaves, and it emotionally tills the soil of our life. The phase of grief can bring out many different behaviors in us that may not make sense to the casual observer, but they are important to us.

I learned that those moments are when you have the opportunity to change the feeling of "old folks' homes" to a great community that supports and serves the whole family. Ultimately, that error had no negative impact on her, and I am grateful for the perspective it gave me. And in fact, that perspective launched a whole new point of view for The Springs Living, which is still committed to making a positive impact for the lives of our customers' families.

All those failures were aspirational promise failures. An aspirational promise is certain to fail, and I proved that principle in spades. In a business that never shuts down or closes its doors and one that encompasses healthcare, hospitality, real estate, management, leadership, human resources, and more, I struggled to get clarity and a grasp of everything that needed completing and how to do it while fulfilling our business and aspirational promises. Having the opportunity to correct those failures drove me forward, toward the problem and a sense that I could make a difference if I only didn't give up.

In the beginning, I had no intention of having a growing senior housing company, nor did I have the intention of making it my career. Our Salem, Oregon, community led to our Clackamas, Oregon, community, which led to our Missoula, Montana, community, and with each iteration we improved. Yet in each iteration we learned, and with that knowledge we wanted to do it again.

It was failures, not the successes, that drove me and gave a sense of mission and purpose in my life. It wasn't about growing a company to make more money or build an empire; I felt compelled to make the lives of the people who were part of our communities better, to make the world of senior housing better. What drove me to grow and expand was the opportunity to do better and the realization that a company, like a person, has to grow or it will die. Whether it was in the design and construction of the building, the operational start-up, or the need to grow in size so we had more resources to invest in operational infrastructure, we kept failing—and learning and evolving and growing.

Instead of this being the end of a fairy tale and the end of this book, the death of Lillian Margaret Stubblefield was the start of this story about a promise unfulfilled. But then again, in a culture of promise, aspirational promises are never done being fulfilled. You are always *aspiring* to more.

> *Vision and clarity are where you start to make a difference.*

I started driving north to a meeting in Seattle. It was a winter day, and I knew it would be slow going, but I just didn't realize how slow. As I passed the exit for Longview on Interstate 5 north, I hit a wall of white. The visibility disappeared along with the cautious fifty miles per hour I had already been driving. Before long, I was barely moving against the blizzard. The defroster and the wipers strained to keep my windshield clear as I slowed to a near stop. Like organizations that are slow to evolve and adapt, stopping for any reason on an interstate is never a good idea. Nor was it a good idea to pull off to the side, as I could get stuck and be trapped for hours. Veering right toward the shoulder while splitting my gaze between straight ahead and my rearview mirror, I felt a bump, and then another and another. I was feeling the raised reflectors in the road. I was driving by braille, and it felt very much like how I was running our business at that time. Like driving in that storm, I felt my way along the route of a growing company, not sure where the path ahead exactly was. Starting the company had seemed so simple. Build a building, hire some good people, and keep a promise—what could be complicated about that?

But now, with four buildings operating and another one under construction, I began to question my decision. A hodgepodge group of passionate people who wanted to change an industry was full of possibility, but the reality of blending all the elements of such an endeavor was uncertain. It's been said that hope is not a strategy, so just like driving in that snowstorm, I slowed the car down and slowed my plans down. I had a vision, but what I needed was clarity on how to connect the dots from the reality of today and the vision of tomorrow—and just when I was looking for clarity, things got even stormier.

The Twin Towers fell, devastating our country and putting my company and the latest project in jeopardy. Move-in reservations stopped, and people who had planned to move into my biggest and most ambitious new community to date, a 143-unit expansion to our existing Springs at Clackamas Woods, canceled. People didn't want to live in communities that terrorists could target. Irrational fear is still fear, and perception frames reality. Occupancy dipped, and staffing was hard. I had hired an operations manager, but he was not making progress. I had to make a hard decision to free up his future and reorganize. I had started the company, but I had never actually worked in the day-to-day operations. I decided that if it was to be, it was up to me, and I took the role of executive director at The Springs at Clackamas Woods, 208 units of independent and assisted living. I was driving by braille.

Purple Hearts for Promise Keepers

My promise had become bigger than just the one to my grandma; now, every time a person moved into one of our communities, I felt I was making a sacred vow to another grandparent. No longer was this promise just to my grandmother but to each person who lived there. I felt the weight and responsibility on my shoulders. I welcomed the burden, like I was made for the task, but the problem was that I had no idea what I was doing.

Like raising a young family, which Julie and I were doing, these welcomed, purposeful responsibilities for others' lives pushed the capacity of our time and talents. No one said living a life of purpose is easy, and I felt about as qualified to parent our young children as I did to run this company. One evening, after the nighttime routine of putting the kids down, Julie and I weighed the decision of raising our young family and running our business. We reasoned that if we were to go broke, we would have a harder time raising our family. Everything we had was in this business. The only direction we could move was toward success. She knew how thin we ran the company, evidenced by my long hours and the sleeping bag I kept under my office desk.

We were about to make one of the best business decisions in our lifetime; we just didn't know it yet. As I look back, that decision seemed so logical, but at that moment, the future was not clear. If I was going to change an industry, I first had to change what was happening in our buildings. I could not allow us to become an old folks' home. *I had a promise to keep.*

Not only did I take over as the executive director, but I moved into the building and filled the role as one of the night managers. It turns out that if you truly want to know what happens in a building twenty-four seven, don't look at a report—move in. Go to shift changes, fill a maintenance request, and eat the food. It won't take long to realize the dedication, care, and hard work it takes.

Unless you have actually worked in the day-to-day operations of a senior housing community for more than a brief training session, you have no idea what goes on each day and each night and therefore no idea how to lead such an organization. I did not grow up working in a care setting, even if at times it felt like it. Lehman was a hospitality operation, although we cared for plenty of guests, and most days it felt like a twenty-four-hour operation. I did not have the education or qualifications to run this business. At the time, I had a partner, Greg, who put up the money to get us going and was counting on me; our employees, our residents, and my own family were looking to me to turn things around. Greg was a great partner and did many things to help us get going but senior housing was not his expertise. If I was going to fail, I would go down with a fight. Looking back, I know that experience of running and living in the community was foundational to the success of our company. Not because I was the best executive director but because I jumped headfirst into a pool filled with problems and had no choice but to swim. The clarity I gained on what goes on in a community is perhaps the most important lesson I could have learned.

The 1980s concept of management by wandering about (MBWA) works well in this setting. But be prepared to not just observe; be prepared to pitch in and lend a hand. The sure thing that can be expected in a retirement community is the unexpected. It's a microcosm of life outside its walls. What happens in a retirement community is kind of like college but with legal drugs and at a much slower pace! Our communities are people's homes where they live, love, have problems, and enjoy celebrations. Wandering the building at two in the morning after a shift changes your perspective. Our staff members have impossible and noble jobs. We are a human version of a supportive device. We support someone's life the way hearing aids support their hearing and walkers support mobility. We become healthcare representatives and amateur psychologists all in one. We are not in the hospitality business, the real estate business, or the healthcare business—we are all these combined into one service. *We are in the service business.*

It takes serving in a building for an extended period of time to earn the badge of honor, like the Purple Heart in the military. You cannot get this special badge by taking a class or even working a shift here or there. To understand the opposite forces that pull and push the life of a care worker takes time. It takes time to put yourself on the front line and be vulnerable. In doing so, you will experience some of the hardest of life's moments in people's lives and equally the most beautiful qualities of human nature. Those who care for others are doves, angels, and saints.

Those who can see past the complaints and problems, who can see past the family members who aren't making the situation better and take it in stride when they are disrespected are a special kind of person. This job gives them a sense of purpose, their mission—one that feeds their sense of worth. In a culture of promise organization, even the chef in the community is a caregiver. Imagine a chef whose customers are disappointed with the food almost daily. You have to understand it's not about the food. Only two possibilities exist: either your food is actually bad and you need to find a new career or you take it as a compliment that they will actually give you feedback. We tend to compare food service in senior housing to our favorite restaurants when the only thing in common between the two is that they serve food. I am not sure many people would rave about their favorite restaurant if they had to eat there for every meal, every day. Combine that with the fact that your customers are older adults, more set in their ways, have physiological changes to their senses like taste, may be taking multiple prescription drugs, and have a lot of time on their hands to be food critics. In addition, if you serve meatloaf, or any dish associated with fond memories for them, the fact is that even your best chef's meals will not compare to memories.

If you don't understand this dynamic, how long do you think it would take before you got discouraged and decided to quit? This is just one example of how to earn a Purple Heart in senior living. And, like in the military, where none can understand combat until they are in it—and when you get wounded you get a Purple Heart—it is also true that no one can understand a culture of promise unless they have lived it. A failed aspirational promise is a wound of honor for those who serve there and deserves to be honored and celebrated even as we work to solve the problem and become better.

Living and working in a building led me to make another promise—that our operations would never be led by someone who had not earned that Purple Heart, a metaphor for having survived on the front lines of our noble profession. When you immerse yourself in what is actually happening in these environments, even today, it becomes easy to see why as an industry we have low satisfaction and high employee turnover. But in a culture of promise, you can never accept mediocrity. You can never give up and must get back in the saddle, fix the problem, learn, and evolve, because the only way to break a promise in a culture of promise is to give up.

I learned that when we had events and activities in the community, the food complaints went down even if we had not made any progress in the quality. I learned that having your customers complain was key to knowing your quality. Because if they ever stop complaining, it means they have given up on you and are likely getting ready to move out. It's actually good to have a high level of feedback. I learned to look for frequency and the type of complaint. Each community has a rhythm, and even the best community should have a steady flow of feedback. Having a complaint that the carrots are not cooked correctly is welcome feedback, but hearing from a family member that their parents hadn't had their shower in weeks is not good! When you really look at what is going on in a building, you see that you have a built-in management and quality feedback structure composed of highly intelligent and experienced people called residents, and those professionals actually pay you to give you feedback. The problem is that we don't see them with that level of respect and thus utilize them to help make the living conditions better. *This point of view, if embraced, will revolutionize your operations.*

There is no way organizations can create quality all by themselves. It takes getting everyone on the same page, working toward a common goal, to do that. Residents and their families are a vital part of creating quality with our staff, and our financial stakeholders must have clarity to support that outcome.

The radio talk show host Dr. Laura famously says to her heartsick callers, "Love is not enough." I have spent many years in the care and service business, and in that time I have met very few people who don't care. I have met a lot of folks who have not chosen their business partners well or employed great strategy or who have gotten complacent and have not continued to learn, grow, and invest in themselves, much less others. The conclusion is clear: "Just to care is not enough." If we are going to fulfill our promises, we need to also have vision and clarity; we need to be part of organizations that have good strategy and good resources. When I started, I had a vision, but I did not have clarity; therefore, I could not have good strategy or resources.

Working in the building, I started to connect clarity to the vision of building best-in-class communities for older adults. I began to see the interdependent relationships among our residents, our employees, and the owners or investors. Our residents need us to fulfill our promise to take care of them. Our employees need us to provide a stable and energizing environment to do their work and take care of themselves and their families. Our investors, vendors, and bankers need us to keep our business promises. And all these groups must understand that quality cannot happen without their participation, alignment, understanding, and trust. I started to connect the dots with three-dimensional clarity.

As I worked and learned and failed over and over, I began to see the successes and failures as a picture starting to emerge, like looking at a stereogram—you know, the picture that looks like the old TVs when they didn't get any reception. When you first look at a stereogram, it seems like a frenetic mess of visual noise in the form of dots with no image at all. But as you spend time and relax your eyes past the immediate static, the real picture emerges, and that is the best way for me to describe what was beginning to happen for me.

I started to see the picture the way our customers see it. The industry, for the most part, was good at getting folks to move into communities, mainly because many did not have a choice. It is also pretty good at getting people to stay in our communities. It has been commonly known that people just don't move out after they move in.

But what I was finally seeing was a clear picture that it was the rare community that went to the next level of service, getting people to find a purpose and live and thrive after they moved in. Haunting were the conversations with our residents who felt their life was over and they were just waiting to die. Yet I knew this did not need to be the case. Life is amazing no matter what the stage; it is just different. We were never going to be satisfied with just high occupancy and financial results. We were never going to be a warehouse for people waiting to die. Our job was to support each resident and their family so that they can stay high on Maslow's hierarchy and wake up each day with something purposeful to look forward to. Merely to accomplish this mission impossible of what our customers needed and wanted was not enough. For us to truly make a difference, we would need to understand and connect with every dimension. The very best workforce was the second dimension, and the right capital partners was the third, and I was about to enter the third dimension.

KEY TAKEAWAYS:

- The move from an independent home to a senior living community, even a nice one, often feels like a loss of independence and can be an emotionally difficult transition.

- Understanding the psychological perspectives like Maslow's hierarchy of needs can help the industry empathize with residents' perspectives and experiences. Residents often feel their life and purpose diminishing as health declines.

- The industry has historically not seen residents as customers and has not sufficiently utilized their feedback to improve quality of life and service.

- Rather than focus solely on occupancy rates and financial metrics, the industry should prioritize supporting residents in continuing purposeful and engaged lives.

CHAPTER 6

Discovering Promise Limiters: Understanding Your Promise

Promises are the uniquely human way of ordering the future, making it predictable and reliable to the extent that this is humanly possible.

—Hannah Arendt

I boarded the early United flight from Portland to Chicago. I was headed to meet Chris Galvin, the cofounder along with Chris Merrill, of Harrison Street Real Estate, a relatively new private equity firm that specializes in investing in senior housing. Mr. Galvin had sold his stock in Motorola, the company his grandfather started on Harrison Street in Chicago in 1925, the same year my grandfather had purchased Lehman Hot Springs. Chris's father had been CEO after his dad, and then Chris had followed in their footsteps, also rising to become Motorola's CEO. Needless to say, I was a little nervous. I had never met a Fortune 100 CEO, much less one who was considering investing in my company.

It was 2009, and the impacts of the Great Financial Crisis, which started in 2007, were still claiming the financial lives of companies and businesspeople. My seed capital partner had found himself in a bit of a financial pickle due to the crisis and was exploring options to raise money, mainly by selling his interests in our company. Our legal documents provided me with the opportunity to buy him out, but there was one problem—I didn't have enough money, not by a long shot. I was being forced out of the business and the company I had started and given my heart and soul to unless I could find another financial backer—and soon. It was at this moment in time that I learned the importance of picking the right financial partner. I always knew that the wrong partner could make a good deal go bad and that a good partner could make a bad deal work out, but now I was living it.

I was lucky on this flight—no one was sitting in the middle seat, so I could spread my financial statements out for review. I have always found flying a good time to focus. If I was going to meet the CEO of a private equity firm, I damn sure was going to know all my numbers. I worked to break down and memorize each community's EBITDA (net operating income), GSR (gross schedule rents), and expenses, and I knew them by unit, by PRD (per resident day), and as a percentage of income, along with other commonly discussed financial indicators. I knew I had one shot to make a good impression.

Upon my arrival at their office high above Wacker Drive and inside the Loop, Chris gestured me into a small conference room off the main office floor, where rows of cubicles housed young aspiring analysts like plastic seedling trays in a greenhouse. His gray hair and distinguished style only enhanced his calm and confident manner.

Hollywood could not have cast a better person for his role in this movie. As our conversation moved past the normal niceties about the ease of my trip and my impression of the hotel they had recommended, I was shifting in my chair, looking for the right posture to convey that I belonged in this room. He launched his first question.

"Tell me about your culture," he said with a warm and sincere tone. The question caught me off guard and made me momentarily freeze like in the childhood yard game of tag. My mental double take slowly sunk in, and his question started to put me at ease like I was slipping into a comfortable pair of shoes. This was not the first question I had anticipated, nor did any of my three-by-five note cards from the airplane cover this topic. I hadn't practiced this answer—but nor did I need to.

"Oh," I said, eyes widening and inhaling a breath that relaxed my posture and put a smile on my face. "That's an easy one," I blurted in a vulnerable response. I launched into the story of my grandma, the people I worked with, and Lehman Hot Springs. My words came and had no need for cue cards or practiced answers. The story flowed out of me like the hot mineral waters of a spring. He listened patiently like a therapist who is trained to get you to look deep into your soul, and then he asked his next question.

"How big do you want to grow?"

My response was immediate. With excessive confidence, I said knowingly, "Oh, I don't want to be big, just the best. Besides," I continued, "this is not a big-company business."

"What do you mean?" he replied.

"Well, from everything I have seen in this business, the bigger the company grows, the worse the quality gets."

"Really?" he questioned, letting the last syllable linger a bit, then he added, "Tell me more." For the next bit of time, I told him my opinion of what I had seen from many of the buildings I had visited and knew about that were owned or managed by what I could consider larger companies. Of course, at that point in time "large companies" included almost everyone but us. I told him my impression that it seemed they prioritized scale over quality and relayed what the working and living conditions were in these buildings from my observation. My final condemnation came when I said, "I wouldn't want to live or work in one, much less put my grandmother in one. I guess I just don't want to build an old folks' home just to make money." My youth and inexperience made me sound like a populist politician railing against the system.

His response conveyed an understanding of the world I could not comprehend in that moment or at my company's stage of development. And then he made a statement that caused the gears of my brain to shift into low range, trying to find traction so I could process his statement. He said, "It's not about the size of the company. It's that you and maybe the industry do not understand its limiters."

"Understand limiters? What do you mean?" For the next few minutes, I felt like I was sitting in a four-hundred-level college class learning about a subject that deeply interested me. He told me the story of his grandfather starting Motorola and the lessons they learned and their invention of Six Sigma (engineer Bill Smith developed it while at Motorola), their way of identifying and expanding their limiters like a component in a computer chip. His historical perspective corrected my misconception—"It was not Jack Welch and General Electric that invented Six Sigma, the process to continually improve quality, but Motorola, " he said, setting the record straight. It felt like he was settling an old score, since most of the business world thought that Six Sigma was GE's way. Jack Welch was the General Electric CEO, and a book *Jack Welch & the G.E. Way,* by Robert Slater, talked about Jack and his implementation of Six Sigma at General Electric. The media conflated it so that many people today still think Welch came up with it.

The meeting must have been successful, because we closed the deal to buy out my old partner and have never looked back. Harrison Street has remained a strategic partner for our company ever since. As important as the deal itself was—it breathed new capital into our growing business—it also ignited my obsession to understand limiters. And thus began my quest with finding the limiters to growing without sacrificing quality. To grow quality we would need to grow business systems, resources, people, and capital to carry the load that growth provides. I wanted to know all the dimensions and their limiters for my own business as well as the industry that was based on a simple promise to all older adults: "We will take care of you."

3D Vision Framework

When we say something is three-dimensional, or 3D, it is defined as the length, breadth, and width—basically being able to see the whole picture. Just like the earth is not flat, neither is your business, and having a map will open up vast new worlds and allow other talented people to join. At this time we owned four communities, and if we grew again, I knew things would have to change—we would need to be at a tipping point to evolve the business with vision statements and taglines and all the things I had learned in college and by reading business books. Having clarity in your organization is perhaps one of the most important things you can do. When I say having clarity, I mean more than just writing a vision or mission statement. I mean seeing your entire business in a simple and concise way even though we know nothing is simple. We cannot effectively write a vision or mission statement until we have the full picture of our customers' needs and the business we are truly in. Likewise, every organization must understand the things that block their growth by understanding the things that limit that growth and then working to expand the capacity of those limiters. What had I learned from living and working in our communities, and how could I create clarity and then a plan to build our organization?

The idea for our 3D framework came as I was obsessed with the concept of limiters that Chris Galvin had planted into my head. If such a concept could propel a great company like Motorola, could it help our company keep its promise? Could I create a framework that simplified the complex nature of promising to take care of people while meeting all of the other demands on a business? For the most part, unless you are creating the next brain surgery breakthrough or mapping the genome, you need to keep things simple by knowing where you are going and then how to get there. In other words, having clarity on how to keep your promises is the key to success. I have always tried to follow the KISS principle to life—you know, Keep It Simple, Stubblefield!

The creators of nursing homes started out trying to solve a problem in America, mainly how to take better care of the elderly. Care needed to be reinvented and evolved once again. After World War II and the emergence of corporate America, the economy boomed, fewer families lived in the same town generation after generation, and those that did had jobs. Women streamed into the workforce, and America needed a solution and owed a debt to the longest-living generations that had taken us through the turn of the century, World War I, and the Great Depression and launched us into the future. Nursing homes or skilled nursing homes were the first iteration of modern long-term care after the passage of The Medicare and Medicaid Act in 1965.

Like the first release of a new piece of software, we seldom get it right the first time. But while computing capacity, defined by Moore's law, doubles roughly every two years, it would be eighteen years until we really got started down the road of version 2.0 of long-term care, the assisted living era.

Today, we find ourselves on the edge of a demographic boom and desperately in need of understanding the limiters to quality in version 3.0 for the great boom ahead. We don't need to simply copy the past like you would using a Xerox machine; we need a whole new approach. If the nursing home era was created in black and white, then the assisted living era was in full color with homelike buildings, less licensed staff, and payers that were for the most part private, not Uncle Sam. What we need today is a fresh new way to look at our industry. We need dynamic framework to take into consideration all the complexities of our medical system and our promise to take care of older adults. It's not a linear problem and needs a 3D assessment to get it to the next version.

As my time living in The Springs at Clackamas Woods and being the executive director came to an end and I once again slept in my own bed seven nights a week, my experience formulated into clarity, concepts, and strategies. The skies cleared, and I was able to accelerate down the freeway. An idea was formulating in my mind, and I was starting to see our customers' needs and our business more clearly.

Our customers' decision to move out of their castle, their home, and into a retirement community was a major life decision. I watched as people spent years doing everything they could to avoid the move. I watched some prospective residents' hope of moving into our independent living community slip away because of indecision. They hung on with everything they had to that top rung of the ladder as age, health, and time eroded their support until they had to let go, metaphorically falling hard down Maslow's hierarchy toward the ground. That fall sometimes ended up in broken hips that sent them to nursing care and not the homelike environment with friends and where family actually enjoyed visiting. In other words, their inability to make a decision ended up causing a slow and painful decline in their health and quality of life.

In the book *Being Mortal,* by Atul Gawande, the author talks about the aging process, where the goal is to live well as long as possible and make the decline as short as possible. This can rarely be done without support when you are an older adult. That means support for basic needs like food and healthcare but also, as or possibly more important, support for the whole person's wellness. Social determinants impact the quality of relationships and health. To support the whole person, older adults face a monumental decision and reality: that they are nearing the end of their time and the issue of how to support their lives in the new reality of frailty in older age. I cannot emphasize how big a decision this is for older adults, many of whom are not at the peak of their mental capacity—a decision to move out of the American dream, their home. The impossible decision is that they know they cannot stay in their burdensome single-family home, which has become their prison, nor can they move somewhere that in their mind is akin to waiting to die. It is an impossible decision for most. For many, moving in with adult children is not an option because of space, distance, or two-income families where no one would be home to care for Mom or Dad.

For our part, an industry mainly operated by younger people not yet past retirement, we hire a marketing person and put them in our buildings to get them to rent apartments. I say "not yet past retirement" because it is a misnomer to call what the senior housing and care industry does as retirement living. Golf every day or moving to the beach is what many think of when we say the word retire. Our customers who need our services and who we support, for the most part, have long passed the stereotypical retirement, yet still retain a zest for life and possess the ability to have valuable contributions to their families, their neighbors, and society. Many even reemerge into the workforce or other useful pursuits living a whole other life past their retirement career and prior to the effects of aging that caused them to seek our support. Yet "retirement" is the label that has stuck to describe this phase of life. As operators, we can fool ourselves to think that if we get a move-in, our job is done. We fail to realize that this first step is just that, a first step. Not looking beyond that first step was the first limiter I discovered.

My company was limited by the lack of understanding of the challenges our customers were going through, which created a lack of understanding as to how to meet their needs. Not only did we not understand the problem, but we didn't understand how to support our customers' quest for continued purpose and usefulness. We hired marketing consultants to give us sales techniques and coach our marketing teams on how to handle the most common of objections, like "I am not ready yet."

The concept of the 3D Framework I created was to help me fully understand the length, the breadth, and the width of our customers' decision-making process and identify the limiters to quality and thus success. The *D* also stands for "decision"; bear with me on this concept, because it has a metaphorical meaning that will become clear soon. Understanding the decision process of all our stakeholder dimensions was my goal.

Making decisions, like eating your dinner, has to be done one bite at a time and takes time. Most people just don't wake up one day and say, "I am going to move into a retirement community." Their decision-making process starts with a journey of curiosity, one step at a time that can take years. Typically, either they or their spouse is having challenges due to the aging process, and their American dream becomes an American nightmare as they cannot keep up with the chores at the house or the demanding caregiving tasks for themselves or their spouse. This is when they make their first call to a community like The Springs. The one thing we know is that when someone calls us and starts inquiring about what we offer, they have a need.

For the most part, we see people fall into two groups: planners and deniers. The deniers likely need immediate help and a higher level of care; the planners can slow the acute decline by getting more support with basic things like meals, housekeeping, and relief from the worry and burden of the home. A good friend and colleague of mine, Phill Fogg Jr., who owns and operates Marquis Companies, calls these two groups the "Oh shit, we need to plan" group and the "God forbid I ever move into a facility" group. He stresses the need for all of us to plan for this phase of life, because there is only one way for each of us to avoid this chapter of life! The 3D Vision was created to help our employees understand our customers' decision-making process in three dimensions. The three dimensions are our customer dimension, our employee dimension, and our capital or investor dimension. The three decisions that need to be made in each dimension are the decision to move, the decision to stay, and the decision to thrive.

3D Vision for Three Stakeholder Groups

What's Good for the Goose

My grandma used to say, "What's good for the goose is good for the gander." Obviously some words of wisdom. As a boy, I never asked her what she meant by that, but I took away the concept of fairness and the idea that if it's good for one, it should be good for all.

Building off the three-dimensional concept, I began to see the full breadth, width, and length of the interrelationship among our three stakeholder groups and what I observed as the three decisions our customers needed to go through to learn to live well for a longer life in our communities. I saw the 3D Vision Framework concept offering a great metaphor, because it stands for fully understanding all the dimensions of your business and your promises—3D because it allows you to clearly see what decisions each of your dimensions or stakeholders need to go through to truly build a successful and stable organization. Understanding your customers' decision-making process can help you craft solutions to meet their needs and fulfill your promises. Using this concept, I realized I could communicate the impact we wanted to make in all our stakeholders' lives.

If your only goal is to make money, this is not the book for you. That is a two-dimensional concept. I am not saying making money is not important—it is. You can't help others if you can't pay your bills and achieve your own self-actualization, however you define that. Paul Klaassen, the Sunrise Senior Living founder, while not his original quote, was well known for saying there is no mission without the margin. Three-dimensional clarity includes making money, but making money is a by-product, not a target. We are not stamping out widgets on a factory floor (nothing against widget makers); as an organization, whether for profit or nonprofit, it's more like planting an orchard. You have to do it right to eventually get apples. Following this process will not only help all your stakeholders thrive in their lives; it will help you thrive too. Like planting an orchard, if you take your time up front and invest in the soil and grow the trees, eventually you will have a recurring crop to pay your bills and support your life. When you focus on fulfilling your promise and making the right organizational investments to ensure your quality, you are planting an orchard of relationships that, when mature, will be able to create value and sustain profits for all stakeholders.

Having the full picture, the 3D Vision Framework helps you understand the stages of your stakeholders like understanding the seasons of the year. All your stakeholders—your customers, the employees, and the investors—gain value from the relationship with your organization, albeit in different ways. Customers take satisfaction from the goods and services you provide at a good value; employees earn support for their lives and dreams in the form of wages, salaries, and bonuses; and investors earn monetary profits, if any are left over, in the form of a return on their capital invested, as well as the knowledge that they are providing a social good. The amount of profit and value gained is directly correlated to the risk each group has for the organization's success. If it is not successful, the customer and employee can leave the investors holding the bag. This interdependence binds the groups to the others and makes it in everyone's interest to maintain a balance of interest, meaning the organization will stumble if the investors are greedy and take too much money out of the organization or do not invest back into their employees, their business systems, R&D, or the customer experience and value.

As I sketched out the 3D Vision Framework concept in my notebook, I started to understand our stakeholders and the dimensions of their decision-making processes. This is what I drew in my notebook:

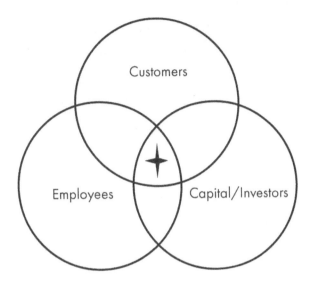

The image shows the three internal stakeholder groups necessary in an organization. In a culture of promise organization, the interests of all these groups must intersect in a way that keeps balance, fairness, and trust. The job of the leaders and the managers of the organization is to balance the interest of all three stakeholder groups (indicated graphically with the star above).

Maintaining balance in an organization takes work and trust. The ways that an organization can get out of balance are many. For example, if the investors decide to take too much capital out of the business, it won't have the financial resources to reinvest or change with the times. If the employees don't pay attention to the residents or are not good stewards of the organization's money, imbalance can occur, leading to problems. With 3D Vision Framework, organizations can stay in balance by understanding the needs of all their stakeholders. To understand the balance, I needed to understand the three decision-making phases of our stakeholders, and the decision-making process is surprisingly similar for all three groups.

I was on my way to my final job interview in the early 1990s. At the time, I was working for a national commercial real estate investment company called Grubb and Ellis. I was considering making a move to a start-up boutique firm made up of some guys who had also been with large national companies. If I accepted the job, I would be their first employee. As I drove to the final interview, I knew that if they asked me to join, I needed to be prepared to answer the question. I was established in my business, but taking this new job could give me a significantly larger opportunity to earn more money and become free of the one-size-fits-all corporate approach, which in my opinion was hindering my business. I told myself that if I ever had my own company, I would create a way for the best and brightest to have more organizational input. But, for now, that was a distant dream.

I stopped in the restroom before entering their company headquarters to check if my tie was straight, since I had a tendency to be a little absent-minded about my personal appearance. I had learned the hard way to double-check myself, because I had done things like wearing a different suit coat with the wrong pants, forgetting the final zips and buttons, and forgetting to comb my hair before I left the house. As I looked in the mirror, I drew a deep breath, and for some reason that moment seared into my memory, like remembering your exact location when you heard some tragic news. "Yes," I told myself. I would take the job. But then I said out loud, "But we will see if I stay."

I had just made the first step in the 3D Vision Framework process: as an employee, I made the *decision to move* to that company. Taking a job or moving into a new place is one decision, but the *decision to stay* in that job or live in a place is made daily. In the end, it was the right decision, and looking back, it was a great move where I learned a lot. I even made it to the second decision to stay, at least for the next four years. Ultimately, I would not make it to the *decision to thrive* there, and I would leave that company in 1996 to start my own dream of reaching the peak of Maslow's hierarchy, which often looked like an unscalable mountain. Similarly, this is the decision process that every customer goes through before moving into one of our communities. It also represents what our capital partners and investors go through in their decision to invest in our company.

The 3D Vision Framework matrix was developed through years of experience and observation of the behaviors of stakeholders in an organization and their process of decision-making. In my experience, most people do not like to make decisions that involve change or are very cautious in doing so. Not moving in, not taking a job, and not investing are all decisions. It's the change in the status quo that is the more difficult decision. By understanding the process, not only can we guide our customers toward good decisions but we can also understand our promises to them and the limiters to keeping those promises. When we understand the limiters, we can take actions that will help us fulfill our promises. Below is where the decision-making steps take place on Maslow's hierarchy:

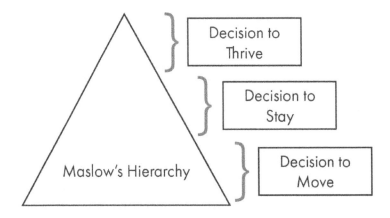

The Decision to Move

Customers can come to any organization from any of the five areas of Maslow's hierarchy. Marketing and sales processes live in the decision to move, where the employee recruiting and the capital raise live. At this level customers engage with your organization in order to seek a solution to their problems or needs. Below are some of the functional areas in our organization that create the messaging to each stakeholder on how we are going to promise to meet their needs.

	Customer	Employee	Investor
Decision to Move	Sales and marketing	Recruiting	Raising capital

If you can't get folks to buy your product or service, take jobs with you, or invest, it's likely you won't be in business very long. But while the decision to move is the easiest to get your customer to say yes to, it's also the first step to understanding what they need, making your promise, and then fulfilling your promise. Simple, right? Plenty of gimmicks and sales techniques exist to persuade people into a sale. We hire likable and charismatic people to sell our products or services, and we arm them with tools, training, and techniques to close the sale. But if we aren't careful, even if we get the sale, we will have set ourselves up for failure if we do not follow a very deliberate process. Just selling is shortsighted; if you aren't sure you can fulfill your promise, you will be doing irreparable harm to your brand. In this phase of the decision-making process, customers are trying to make a decision to say yes or not. You know that they have either a need or a desire just from the fact that they contacted you. The question is, do you offer the right solution for them? Anytime someone calls us on the phone, makes an online inquiry, or pops into one of our communities just to look around, they are telling us they have a need.

It's our job to make sure we can fulfill the need. This is the difference between just selling someone and making them a promise. For the most part, the sales department is looked at as transactional. Salespeople get paid based on the number of sales, not on whether the product actually meets the need. In a culture of promise, you aren't selling; you are making promises to those whom you believe you can help. For that to be successful, the salespeople must be sure that the organization can fulfill its promise, or the sale will actually undermine the culture and the organization. Typically, this decision to move falls to your sales and marketing teams. However, you have to make sure those teams are setting the customer up to make the next two decisions, to stay and to thrive.

What I like about using this framework to get people through this first-step decision is that it breaks down the process into manageable steps and helps us think about our customers, our employees, and our business all at the same time. In this decision-to-move phase, for your customers, you might have decision goals as follows:

The Decision-to-Move Goals

Decision-to-Move Goal 1. Accurately understand, identify, and verify the customers' individual needs (Maslow). What problem are you solving for them?

Decision-to-Move Goal 2. Make sure the organization can fulfill their needs. We don't want someone to move in if we cannot fulfill our promises. Sales folks have great pressure to fill buildings, but one of the worst things you can do is take someone your care team cannot care for. That is like selling someone a ticket to fly on your airline when you don't have anyone qualified to fly the airplane.

Decision-to-Move Goal 3. Just help them to make the decision to move. Don't get in too much of a hurry or overpromise. In the Move and Thrive phases, we will focus on the next steps. If you can get them to say to themselves in that inner voice, "OK, I will move in," that is actually not the best thing. But if you do this right, they will also say to themselves, "OK, I will move in, but I am not sure I will stay." They will be skeptical and wait to see if you can fulfill your sales promise. In senior housing, our customers have seen every tin man for seventy-plus years, so they will usually have realistic expectations for the most part. All you need to do in this phase is get them through those first decision goals. If you do that, you have accomplished the first step of fulfilling the promise. Remember, you eat the apple one bite at a time.

Decision-to-Move Goal 4. Prepare them to think about the next decision: the decision to stay in your community.

For many years we have known that when folks move into our communities, in the vast majority of cases their health improves after a few months. Then, misdiagnosing the root cause of their health improvement, the robust support they now receive, they often look to move back into their home! Clearly they have not made the decision to stay. A recent NORC research study in conjunction with the National Investment Center validates these health improvement outcomes, as detailed in the September 2023 issue of *Senior Housing News*.[6] Making your residents and their families aware of this can help them make the decision to stay. When you get your customers to make the first step, the decision to say yes to moving or trying it out, it relieves the pressure to oversell and make a lifetime commitment

---

6   Lois A. Bowers, "NIC NORC Study Shows Senior Living Communities Make Residents Less Vulnerable," *Senior Housing News*, September 26, 2023, https://seniorhousingnews.com/2023/09/26/nic-norc-study-shows-senior-living-communities-make-residents-less-vulnerable/.

with just one decision. Build your sales process to just get them to that first step—the decision to move.

Now, on your own, walk through what your process might be to get your employees to make the decision to move. Then, do the same thing for the other stakeholder groups you need for your organization to move, like capital providers, before you move on toward understanding how you will get them to make the next decision: the decision to stay.

The Decision to Stay

This phase of your customers' decision-making process is where your customers learn to trust your organization and learn if you really mean what you say. Functionally, it's where your customer fulfillment lives, but emotionally it is where trust that you will fulfill your promise is established. This is the basic operating system and tasks you need to do well just to keep your doors open. Here, you manage your promises for Maslow's hierarchy, all the way from physiological to the level right below self-actualization.

The table below shows where your functional organizational process lives for each stakeholder dimension:

	Customer	Employee	Investor
Decision to Stay	Customer fulfillment systems and processes	Payroll, human resources	FP&A, accounting, investor relations

Customer fulfillment includes your maintenance department that keeps the building looking good, housekeeping that keeps the place clean, the food service department that provides meals and service, health services that tackle the care coordination, and the life enrichment department that works to fulfill the social needs. If you are in a retail business, your goal in this phase of the customer experience is for them to be happy enough not to return the merchandise. In a senior housing community, your goal is to do the basics well enough so that your customer does not want to move out. I have seen a lot of folks move into our communities and know that it takes a lot of screwups for them to move out, so this bar is just not that high, and that is unfortunate. The culture of promise's goal is to make sure you are fulfilling all your brochure promises. Hot food needs to be hot and cold food, cold, and all food needs to be tasty and nutritious. Our team takes this priority seriously and works hard to make it a reality.

Being good at getting your stakeholders through the first two decision processes qualifies you as a successful financial model. However, the 3D Vision Framework process allows you to go a step further and be a promise model. That next step, the decision to thrive, will take your entire organization to the next level of stability, satisfaction, and long-term profitability.

All your fulfillment departments live in this decision. If we do our job here, then the next stage may be our customers saying to themselves, "OK, so I moved in and I think I will stay, but I am not sure I am able to thrive here." Many are resigned to wait out their lives. Some do not expect much, while others expect the universe. Many of our customers are suffering from depression due to many factors like aging and medications. Their friends and family have passed, and they know their time is limited. It is easy for a fatalistic perspective to take over their thoughts and therefore their actions. Some become cranky and old, not afraid to pass along their perspective of hopelessness and misery. Getting people to make the decision to stay is the necessary step toward the ultimate goal of giving people the opportunity to thrive. Walking customers through the decision to stay might look like this:

Decision-to-Stay Goal 1. Make a good handoff from your sales department to your customer relations team.

Decision-to-Stay Goal 2. Make sure you get to know the resident's and their family's expectations and needs. If your sales department oversold them, now is the best time to re-set expectations. If you don't, you are about to have a problem.

Decision-to-Stay Goal 3. The third decision goal is to make sure you establish clear customer communication methods and expectations. This can be done by internal or third-party communication tools like apps or simple text or email protocols. In real estate, the most important three words are location, location, location. In operations the three most important words are communication, communication, communication.

After aligning expectations, getting to know your customer, and establishing a communication plan, you are set up to move to the final phase, which is where you will have the opportunity to excel. Again, repeat this process for your employees and other organizational stakeholders. In a culture of promise, your next goal is to move all three groups toward the decision to thrive.

The Decision to Thrive

	Customer	Employee	Investors
Decision to Thrive	Life enrichment department Purpose, planning and life engagement	Career, planning, training, and education	ESG, superior risk-adjusted returns Providing for the Social Good

Understanding what it takes for our stakeholders (customers, employees, and investors) to thrive is where all the difference can be made. It is in this phase that we cease being an old folks' home, and simply a business. Building on the foundation of the decision to move and the decision to stay, our ultimate purpose is to work to give each of our residents the opportunity to make the choice to climb back up Maslow's mountain to self-actualization.

Ralph Waldo Emerson wrote, "It is to be useful, to be honorable, to be compassionate, to have it make some difference that you have lived and lived well." Realizing that this phase of life for older adults can be just as meaningful as all the other phases changes everything. Gone is the sense of despair at being old; gone is the hopelessness that no good life can happen again until the other side. Life is life and can be lived with satisfaction even in our last chapters. This is where we break back into the principle of self-actualization. This is the real value proposition and goal for every person who moves into senior housing. Realizing that attitude between your ears is the place where a quality of life is lived is like a cool rain on a hot day. The goal in this phase is to get people to Live Life to its Fullest, the tagline for The Springs Living, and embrace their purpose and usefulness in this valued stage of life. When someone moves in and lives in our communities and then realizes they can make a difference in other lives and be of use—that is when they can really thrive. Every action we take is to get our residents to realize that life was not over when they moved out of their single-family home; it was just the beginning of another chapter. This chapter can be lived well, or the time can be squandered in quiet desperation waiting to die. By focusing our organizations on creating environments and on the people to encourage this chapter of life is how we fulfill the promise, never giving up when we are faced with failures or difficulties.

It is in the pursuit of purpose where we find those moments that make it all worth it. Faith Hill, the country-and-western singer, sang of the purpose of life: "The purpose of life is a good cup of coffee, the purpose of life is keeping your eye on the ball." It is such a simple truth that our purpose and satisfaction are not found in grand accomplishments or in defying the gravitational forces with immortality but rather in the simple things. You can make someone's life meaningful and enriched by sending them a big smile, taking time to listen, and giving an appropriate hug. The genuine connection and human contact can make all the difference, because our soul never ages and love never fails. When we structure our organizations for all three stakeholders to thrive, we can make all the difference and change an industry from one where no one wants to move in to one where people can't wait to get old enough to move in!

3D Needs (Maslow)

The needs that each of our stakeholders' dimensions have can be easily seen using our table:

3D Maslow Needs	Customers	Employees	Investors
Decision to Move	Physiological, safety and security, love and belonging	Physiological, safety and security, love and belonging	Safety and security
Decision to Stay	Physiological, safety and security, love and belonging	Physiological, safety and security, love and belonging	Physiological, safety and security, love and belonging
Decision to Thrive	Self-esteem and self-actualization	Self-esteem and self-actualization	Self-actualization

Using Maslow and 3D we can gain an academic understanding of the needs of our stakeholders. In more practical everyday terms, we can then use Maslow's concepts to understand how to meet those 3D needs.

3D Needs	Customers	Employees	Investors
Decision to Move	Social, wellness, food preparation, transportation, security, quality, housing, care coordination, relationship management around the aging process.	A compensation package that meets their needs with salary and benefits. That the organization cares about its residents and employees.	That their inital investment is in an organization that will safely steward their financial resources and create agreed-upon returns.
Decision to Stay	Execution of what you promised and a willingness to listen and solve problems; respect of their autonomy and choices.	Verification that the organization cares and is willing to listen and provide people with respect, appropriate levels of autonomy, and that they can contribute to the whole.	That they get financial results with risk-adjusted returns.
Decision to Thrive	Support for self-discovery and purpose. That they have positive encouragement, quality relationships, usefullness and purpose. That the organization has a purpose they can be proud of because it stewards their resources well.	That they trust that the organization cares about them, their family, and their career; that there are opportunities for growth that help achieve life goals. That they trust that the organization cares about those who it has entrusted to care for.	That their capital contributes to outcomes that help all parties and the environment (DEI and ESG are examples of their goals); that financial performance consistently meets or exceeds expectations.

But to be effective, we need to put these needs into everyday common language to gain an accurate perspective of what our stakeholders need. The perspectives of each of our stakeholders is in the 3D Vision matrix. We need to know what our customers are really saying to themselves, not what they are overtly telling us in each stage of decision-making. Below is what we believe our stakeholders are really saying as they move through the decision-making process:

3D Perspectives	Residents	Employees	Investors/Bankers
Decision to Move	"I will move in, but I am not sure yet if I will stay."	"I will take the job because I need the money, but we will see if I stay."	"We will invest or make a loan, but we will wait to see if they deliver on their promises."
Decision to Stay	"OK, they are doing enough that I will stay."	"I will stay here for now because I have security and safety, but I have bigger dreams."	"The relationship meets the hurdle to continue to do business, and we want to keep doing business."
Decision to Thrive	"I have purpose here and relationships I enjoy, and I want to thrive and help others thrive!"	"I will build my career here because it fulfills my purpose in life."	"We are part of changing an industry, and through our investments we are not only earning a return but helping others live well."

It turns out that our employees and our investors go through a similar decision-making process, and understanding these decisions can help us have clarity, which is needed if we are going to fulfill our promises. Notice how the statements in each decision box are very similar to those of the other stakeholders. You can test the validity of this yourself. Try to recall a job you took where you needed the job, likely for the money. Didn't you say to yourself, at least with an inner voice, "I will take the job, but we will see if I stay"? Or "This company looks good, but you can never know until you see what they are really about."

Understanding the Whys

Beyond understanding the decision-making process of our stakeholders, we can use the 3D Vision Framework matrix in virtually every facet of our business to create clarity and understand promises and problems. Why do my customers pick up the phone? This is your core value to them. Believe it or not, no one actually calls your business for fun. They call because they think you can do something for them and that something will solve a problem or create an opportunity for them. In one sentence, boil down what you believe is your customers' "why."

In our company, our promises to each stakeholder at each stage of the decision-making process are listed in the table below:

3D Vision Promises	Customers	Employees	Investors
Decision to Move	Life is just a little easier here. We care about you and will care and support you.	We pay you, and we offer benefits and a good organizational culture and values.	We will hit our investment targets and run a professional organization.
Decision to Stay	We will work every day to offer a great place to live, and when there is a problem, you can count on us to do the right thing. We will do the chores so you can focus on the relationships.	We will support you, encourage you, and help you grow. If problems arise, we will treat you with dignity, fairness, and respect.	We can grow our organizational capacity to create more opportunity and make your investment more profitable.
Decision to Thrive	We want you to thrive and will support your life purpose or work to help you find your purpose if you don't have one anymore.	We will invest in you and help find your purpose and help you toward your life goals. We support your connection and belonging.	We will work to be a trusted partner that fulfills our promises as we work to make our corner of the world better.

Don't let perfection get in the way of "good enough for now." Momentum is key in any organization, not perfection. You don't need to hire an anthropologist to help you detail each of your nine promise boxes in the 3D matrix. While that would be great, you and your leadership team should be able to get pretty close on your own. In a culture of promise, your one giant goal is to fulfill your promises.

What Are Your Limiters?

Both your business and aspirational promises are bound to fail at some point, and it's the role of every person who works in an organization to hunt down those failures and fix them quickly. Of course, if you know where to look for the problems, it makes it a little easier. Those fails, the problems, are most likely to occur in the areas of your business that limit you. Focusing your efforts on finding problems in these limiter areas and building systems and processes to detect promise breaks will help you solve organizational problems as well as expand those limiters, which will allow you to grow.

Unless you constantly work to expand your limiters to fulfill our promise of quality, you will find that your entire organization and opportunities will be unable to grow, both in size and quality. Using the 3D matrix will help you make sure you fully consider all your stakeholder groups and find problems and areas that could constrain your opportunity. Understanding this on three different levels takes our understanding to a whole new level. You need to understand this for your entire industry, your individual organization, and yourself. Only then, with three-dimensional clarity, can you begin a process of understanding your limiters and growing your quality in your industry, your business, and your own life.

Below are examples of what some of our industry limiters could be:

3D Limiters (Senior Housing and Care)	Customers	Employees	Investors
Decision to Move	Lack of trusted data of the value the sector can add to someone's life over a single-family home. Financial certainty that customers will have enough money. Quality comparisons across providers.	Reputation for low pay and difficult working conditions. Perception and clarity for career opportunities.	No trusted data or transparency through industry reporting. Historical operating data. No confidence in the degree of certainty for financial returns.
Decision to Stay	Not fulfilling the promises given when they moved in. Not listening, lack of follow-through, lack of consistency and not fixing little problems. Frequently changing community leadership and employees.	Running short staffed, lack of nurses, scanty benefits. The perception that companies care more about the profit than the residents and their quality. No clear career paths that can support their life.	The low number of quality providers that allow investors to have confidence to provide capital to the sector. Excessive variability in financial returns.
Decision to Thrive	Lack of appropriate capital structures committed to getting and keeping quality. Short-term management.	Limited understanding of workforce stability and investment into career paths. Perceived bad leadership.	Unsophistication of operators that can further investors' need for ESG. Low understanding of how they are returns of capital or social good.

Every organization and industry needs a vision to understand how to evolve by expanding the constriction of its limiters.

The clarity you get by using the 3D promise process can change your business. Once you understand what your customers truly need from you, you can craft your promise to them and your own system for measuring the fulfillment of those promises. Now, you just need to point your organization in the right direction and lead it forward. And for that you need vision!

KEY TAKEAWAYS:

- Understanding the "limiters" to quality and growth is critical—these are the business systems and resources that constrain scale and improvement.

- Balancing the needs of key stakeholder groups—residents, employees, and investors—is essential to create a sustainable organization and fulfill promises.

- Resident complaints should be encouraged and are opportunities to improve. Lack of complaints likely means residents have given up providing feedback.

- Investing in employees' growth and purpose aids retention and quality performance needed to meet resident needs.

- Providing quality supportive environments for residents to continue purposeful, engaged lives should be the priority—not occupancy rates or financials alone.

CHAPTER 7

This Way, Everybody!

The art of communication is the language of leadership.

—James Humes

Every organization needs direction, and every organization needs a group of leaders aligned with a purpose, a mission, and a plan. At forty thousand feet in the air, the details on the ground seem small. At that altitude, you can start to see the curvature of the earth. For me, working through the 3D Vision process helped me see the world of possibilities and gain a greater understanding of my business and industry. There is a saying in aviation that taking off is optional, but landing is not. To get from point A to point B, you need a plan. In aviation it's called a flight plan; in an organization it's called a business plan. In each circumstance, everyone involved must be clear on where you are going and how to get there. This is the process where you plan to the point of extreme clarity where you are going and why you are going there. The one thing you must do on any flight is land—safely;

otherwise, it's kind of a problem. Promises are like airplanes and pilots like leaders. They have to land at some point, and the better you understand your equipment, the mission, your abilities, and the external factors like weather, the better.

Organizations need a "this way, everybody" statement. As leaders we must clearly set direction by providing the why, what, how, and when. It must be simple and clear for all the stakeholders. It might be in the format of a vision statement, a purpose statement, a mission statement, or a goal, or it might include all of these. Business schools, business consultants, and business books have numerous formulas and formats to choose from. It doesn't really matter which method you use, but you need to use one. Like a target you are aiming for or a race you are running, you must have an aiming point. Countries and cultures have used flags, statues, and statements to symbolize their purpose and culture. It doesn't matter how you do it, just that you must have a clear headline that binds all the people in your organization to a common direction. This drives your culture along with your values and the people you choose to work with.

This vision concept is not rocket science, and most of us do this routinely. Many people are passionate about the formula and feel you must have a vision statement, a mission statement, or a purpose statement. I don't think what you call it is that important nor whether you have just one of those directional and value-grounding statements, but you need to have one or all of these if you want a strong culture. Cultures are linked and defined by a common story and a common language. Common language binds together cultural norms, provides a sense of belonging, and gives that culture an efficiency in communication. Think of a country; if you speak English, French, or Chinese, each language sets a different experience, defines food, traditions, and work ethics. Even in a great melting pot, like America, and in every single organization that has ever existed, they must choose which language will be their go-to for communication. Likewise, each organization must develop its own common language that reflects its cultural beliefs.

You cannot overcommunicate in your organization, and the easier you make your common language, the faster you can grow your quality. Organizational language takes time. When an organization starts out, it's filled with a bunch of people who worked at other places. All that "other place" experience comes together to create and solve, and when this happens your teammates offer up suggestions by stating "how we did it there." That is all well and good until you need to start maturing and coalescing as an organization. Then you will need to turn the "how we did it there" statements to "how we do it here" systems, policies, and language to begin the curation of your organizational culture. Franchise companies have already done most of this work for you, especially with the systems and policies. They can even help you jump-start your culture, but even with that kind of head start in a company, you will still need to form your unique language and culture. Creating this vocabulary and language is an organic process and takes time.

I started my company in 1996, and I didn't start to formally begin to create our cultural and operating systems until 2004, eight years later. I do not recommend waiting that long, and that is one of the reasons I wrote this book.

We started that process by realizing we needed to have a big directional statement to get us rowing in the same direction. Today, we say, "This way, everybody" with the acronym PMP. In our company, PMP says it all: Purpose, Mission, Plan.

P stands for Purpose: Your purpose is what drives you. It's an indication of your values, and it's the thing your organization desires more than anything else. This is your forty-thousand-foot view of the world. It needs to be big, genuine, and aspirational, because it shows your direction in the world. If it is authentic, it will build trust, because your stakeholders will see it in every decision you make in the business.

> *Our purpose is this:*
> *to help our residents, their families, our staff, and*
> *each other live life to its fullest.*

A purpose statement reveals the why behind your promise. For us it has a sincere and deep meaning. It links all our stakeholder groups, our residents and their families, our staff, and our investors, bankers, and other vendors together and is consistent with the 3D Vision. All these groups are important to us. Another way you could say it is that we want a "win-win-win" for everyone. It's our grand way of saying that we care, that we understand 3D promises, and that it's our job to fulfill our promises. The key elements for a purpose statement are as follows:

1. It concisely tells everyone your why and indicates your core values.

2. It must be a big, grand, and high-level statement that can connect emotionally to your stakeholders.

3. It has to be authentic to your story and organization.

M stands for Mission: With this statement we are descending a little closer to the ground. Your mission statement needs to be something that ties you to your actual industry and product or service.

This is a ten-thousand-foot view; you are closer to the ground where details become clearer.

> *Our mission is this:*
> *to change the way people think, feel, and experience*
> *senior living.*

This mission statement is tied directly to our promise not to "put me in an old folks' home." This authentic statement is in direct response to the promise I made to my grandmother. The important thing in a mission statement is to connect to the emotions and common purpose of your employee stakeholders. If someone does not understand this, it will take them longer to connect to the organization. This is a "change the world" statement. It is made with the perspective I have outlined in previous chapters and is an understanding that the nursing home era created a stigma that a significant number of people understand and are put off by. Our mission statement changes that. When you write a mission statement, it must check the following boxes:

1. It must be tied directly to your promise, the problem you are solving for your customers. This is your "what."

2. It needs to be authentic to your organization and your culture. It does not need to be eloquent or sweeping (not that it can't be); it just needs to be you.

3. To the maximum extent possible, it should have an emotional connection for your team. It's a rallying cry you will need in the battle of business when you reach those moments when everything goes the wrong direction.

4. It must be simple enough that it can be remembered and repeated by everyone in your organization. This one statement is a daily reminder of what you are doing for your customers.

P stands for Plan: Your plan statement is a simple statement that communicates to all your stakeholders your strategy, your competitive focus to fulfill your promise. This is your "how" statement. Your plan statement is how you are going to land the plane. And when I say "land the plane," I mean fulfill your promise by accomplishing your mission.

> ## Our plan is this:
> *to change the way people think, feel, and experience working in senior living.*

It's a simple concept: to impact quality in a community, you need to impact the people who work there. For us, this plan statement reminds us daily that if you have the best employees, you will likewise attract all the customers you need. It means that if we are a great employer, we will be able to fulfill our promise. This statement tells our stakeholders that we understand where the magic happens in our organization, and that is in the daily interactions among those of us who are directly involved with our customers. The elements I think are important in a plan statement are the following:

1. It must be simple and focuses your stakeholders on the how of fulfilling your mission with the values indicated by your purpose statement—simply a statement of how you fulfill your promise.

2. It must be able to be memorized by all your stakeholders.

3. It should be crafted to have an "oh yeah" effect on employees, meaning that it reminds the leadership of your strategy instead of getting lost in the minutia of daily details.

With these three statements crafted and adopted, you are able to get into your specific and detailed strategy documents, your "how we do it here" statement. I don't need to go into the details of how to do this because many authors have written books on how to create strategies to accomplish your plans. One particular book that I believe reflects what we do on a routine basis is *The Advantage,* by Patrick Lencioni. In his book, he used the concept of Thematic Goals, which is his road map for leading people and being able to say, "This way, everybody."

The concept of 3D Vision and our promises combined with our PMP has taken our organization in a powerful direction, but to execute the plan part of PMP, we needed to be clear on our strategy of how to execute that plan.

KEY TAKEAWAYS:

- Organizations need a "this way, everybody" statement. As leaders we must clearly set direction by providing the why, what, how, and when.

- This vision concept is not rocket science, and most of us do this routinely.

- Communication across the organization can't be overemphasized. Establishing common language and terminology accelerates quality and culture development.

- Your purpose is what drives you. Your mission statement needs to be something that ties you to your actual industry and product or service.

- Your plan statement is a simple statement that communicates to all your stakeholders your strategy and your competitve focus to fulfill your promise.

CHAPTER 8

Distilling a Culture of Promise

The most effective way to do it, is to do it.

—Amelia Earhart

I stared in disbelief at my computer screen. I had punched "Fancho Stubblefield" into my Toshiba laptop. It was 1996, and Google didn't exist yet. The FTP site was slow to react as the modem screeched through the telephone line and sent that odd order of letters, Fancho Stubblefield, into the World Wide Web. The time between hitting the enter key and waiting for the search result to deliver a verdict felt like a wrinkle in time, full of vulnerability. Like the pause before a fortune teller speaks while looking at your hand. I had always been curious about my unusual name, its origins, and the history behind our family that had taken a four-hundred-year journey from Cambridgeshire, England, to Oregon. When the search icon stopped spinning, there was a line of highlighted text titled "Bureau of Prohibition, Seattle, Washington, 1267-M Stubblefield, Fancho, Box 24." I was confused.

What was this? This had to be a mistake; after all, my dad was a deacon in the church. Were we moonshiners?

As reality slowly permeated my mind, the realization that my grandfather Fancho was a moonshiner during Prohibition started to slowly deconstruct my certainty about who I was and where I came from. This new information started a crack in the foundation of my elevated morality built by my teetotaling parents who took us to church three times a week. That search of the World Wide Web was a turning point, expanding my knowledge and course correcting my worldview.

When my grandfather purchased Lehman Hot Springs, Prohibition had been going for five years, making it illegal to sell and consume alcoholic beverages in the United States. Then came the Great Depression, creating an acute focus on putting food on the table. Fancho chose to use the waters of Lehman Hot Springs to make a living in a different way than simply selling swims and hamburgers. He chose to make moonshine. The spring waters of Lehman and the surrounding areas, perhaps combined with the barley harvested by my great-grandfather and grown on reservation land just outside Pendleton, would have been two of the ingredients needed to make moonshine. I had heard rumors of a still at Lehman somewhere in the past, the system and processes needed to take raw materials and use heat, pressure, and time to create the moonshine whiskey. Like a puzzle piece set aside for later, it would take me some time to process and understand how this history would fit into my life other than being a good story to tell sitting around a campfire.

Every organization has a culture, just like every person has DNA. In people we call it personality, but in organizations we call it culture, like an organizational recipe. Emerson famously wrote in his essay "Self-Reliance," "Imitation is suicide." If your competitors are trying to copy your culture, you have nothing to fear. They have already lost or are at least well off the pace. It is only when organizations can be truly authentic and know themselves, like a personal journey of self-discovery, that they can truly fulfill their promise and see their organization thrive to make a difference in the world. Listen to yourself more than the experts, especially consultants, when building your organizational culture. Consultants can give you processes and ideas, but they cannot create your culture for you. That must be authentic to your organization. The best thing you can glean from this book is the confidence to be yourself and embrace your journey and your why. Use the processes and adapt them to build your own story and organization.

Discovering the Power of Values

Barbara and Stanley were waiting in the lobby as the automatic doors at The Springs at Clackamas Woods closed behind me with a gentle swoosh. "Can we talk to you for a minute?" they asked, their body language indicating they knew I was very busy and not wanting to bother me. "Of course," I said as I smiled and hugged Barbara. "How are you guys?" My genuine inquiry opened the door they were waiting for.

Barbara and Stanley had moved from their dream house in the same neighborhood where I'd built The Springs at Clackamas Woods about a year earlier. They were still working through that bittersweet transition between their single-family home and their apartment at The Springs. Our opening was perfectly timed with their need to move out of a home that had become too much to handle, a burden, and not the reprieve it had once been. They had moved just a block away and still enjoyed strolling down their old street and visiting longtime neighbors. Yet adjusting to living in a multifamily setting where neighbors were a wall away instead of over the fence had taken time. They loved our community but had some concerns about some of our leadership.

"Fee," Stanley said, using my first name, which set up the conversation between familiars and trusted friends. "If you could just be here more …"—a statement that told me decisions and practices were not being made by our employees consistent with our promise. The statement absorbed into my mind and sank deep into my heart, like putting on a heavy backpack that instantly weighed me down and made my steps more labored. *If I could just be here more!* The words echoed in my head, like the ringing in the ears after experiencing a loud noise. The problem was that I was hearing this from more than just Stanley and Barbara. I was hearing it from other residents at other Springs communities.

In those early days of the company, I knew most every resident and employee. As I traveled around to see what our teams were doing taking care of folks, I spent a lot of time listening, mainly to suggestions, otherwise known as complaints, and just making people feel heard. The simple reassurance that everything is going to be OK, that we hear you, and that your opinion matters can go a long way. As we grew, and as I had to spread my time over a growing number of communities, invariably, upon visiting a community where I hadn't been in a couple of weeks or more, certain residents and employees would pull me aside in the dining room or hallway and say, "If you could only be here more." Their assumption was that if I was there more, things would be better. Their assumption was inaccurate, because the people we had in the community were far more qualified in their specific jobs than I was, but the residents needed to "feel" that. For someone working in a community, the repetitive complaints about this meal or that can slowly drive you insane, like a steady drip from a sink echoing in a quiet house as you are trying to fall asleep. I had seen it over and over as tenured employees who cared either became calloused or left the industry. There had to be a better way.

I was hearing that same statement from different residents and their families in different communities. Were they conspiring? I was about to scream. I couldn't be there more, not if I wanted to see my kids grow up and not get divorced. As much as I wanted magical powers to expand the time or clone myself, it wouldn't happen. Yet I couldn't help thinking that I was missing something.

I remember exactly where I was when a little voice inside my head said, "You can't be there twenty-four seven, but your values can." That wise voice then said: "Values never sleep, but you have to."

"What does that mean?" I yelled out loud over the music playing on the FM radio in my car. A calm and collected inner voice answered, *"It means you need to hire values, not people."*

At the time, we had huge swings in the quality of our operations. We were small and lacked systems and infrastructure to guide employees. Further, it seemed the systems we did have were never uniformly followed, and we ended up making the same mistakes and missteps over and over again even though I knew we had a binder somewhere with a procedure telling everyone exactly how to do this or that. Even when we had the written systems and spent time training them, no one seemed to follow them with a high degree of accuracy. Not only that, but we kept hiring people who would not treat our residents or their peers with kindness and respect. Managers we hired were inconsistent. Some were controlling and used positional power while frontline staff learned to game the system. However, we always had a number of leaders and frontline people who went the extra mile. Why? The inner voice seemed to be suggesting that if I hired values that came embodied in humans, I might have more success. I had learned through trial and error that I could not train values.

The values of everyone we hired were already intact and had grown from people's parents, ministers, coaches, friends, and families. People either had them or they didn't.

My grandfather used a still to produce moonshine, so why couldn't I use the same concept too? But I would build a distiller to find and attract values into our organization.

Early on, I learned that we were not looking to hire just anyone. We were looking to hire people who really care. Through trial and error, we had allowed some people to work with us who were simply not that nice. What we learned is that like attracts like, meaning that if you hire people who are not nice, eventually they will run off the employees who *are* nice, and then all you will be able to hire is grumpy people, and those people will eventually run off all your good customers. We learned that we needed a way of selecting people who really cared about what we did.

The Ingredients

The ingredients for your organizational recipe are right in front of you. Just the fact that you are reading this book puts you at the top of the class because you have the desire to learn and grow. You have the want to, and that is where everyone starts—it's a required ingredient. Your personal history, the connection of events in your life, your family background, however neatly packaged or messy, are all a part of that recipe. Your education—or lack thereof—is an ingredient. Your work experience, no matter how insignificant you think the job, will play a role in your journey. Next, mix in your values to articulate a solution to a problem. Values, as we have previously discussed, are foundational to the distillation process. Your organizational culture must use shared values, and those shared values must support your customer promise. Your values attract the like-minded people you will need to work with along the way. Values are so important because they determine how we behave, and how we behave is the only thing that matters to our customers, not your intentions.

The Process

The process to create your organizational culture can be developed from your MBA classes or an abundance of business books like this one or Michael E. Gerber's MBA for the working man, *The E-Myth*. Organizational consultants exist around every corner and can provide information and help along the way. Use these sources and your past experiences to create your own processes, like my grandfather created his still to brew his shine so many years ago. These business processes are your "still." Mix in the ingredients, and now you are ready to turn on the heat.

After I discovered my grandfather's adventures as a moonshiner, I opened an email from my second cousin, Kendra Rychlick, then a law student at the University of Washington. I had asked her to file a Freedom of Information request with the Seattle office of the federal government for file 1267-M Stubblefield. The pages contained letters of correspondence between the Umatilla County sheriff, the county where Lehman Hot Springs is located, and the federal officer located in Seattle, commonly known as a revenuer, back during that time. The shocking story revealed in those files is a story for another time and possibly another book. But the information allowed me to piece together the details that would eventually lead me to understand not only what happened but where it happened. Fancho had chosen a location for the still that had abundant water and lots of timber to use for fuel. "Keeping the fires burning" was the name of the game in the moonshine business.

Turn Up the Heat

Heat is needed to make moonshine by distilling the ingredients and building pressure. Heat is also needed to mature an organization. That heat in organizational development is fueled by the determination, passion, and belief in your mission to fulfill your promise. Build the fires of determination, passion, and drive, and your "still," your business processes, will begin the distillation process. As you mix in the elements of running a good organization, the heat will cause natural reactions, and pressure inside the still will build. In your organization, you can feel this pressure. Just as by-products are expelled from the still, so it is with organizations. In organizations, that pressure comes in the way of problems and obstacles. Problems and obstacles are to be embraced as indicators that your distillation process of promise fulfillment is working. Run to those problems, adjust the still, and relieve excess pressure by fixing problems, creating systems, and adapting your strategy.

Adjust your business like adjusting the flame and heat in a still. Practice until you see the value of every success and every failure. I get a smile when business owners feel worried about people copying their ideas or business plans. Unless you are inventing something that needs a patent or have some proprietary IP, I do not think organizations should expend much energy on locking away their best ideas and tying their best talent up with noncompetes and golden handcuffs. Especially in a culture of promise, where people are your key to delivering on your promise, ideas should be shared. No one can be you or be your organization if you follow the principles in this book—in other words, the ways you apply them are unique to the lifeblood of your organization. When you live and work authentically focused on fulfilling your 3D Vision promises, you are unstoppable—just make sure you have all the ingredients and a good strategy. More than enough success is available when you live to fulfill your promises. I heard a market analyst explain the concept of "make share" or "take share" when evaluating if there is enough demand to add supply. Her point was that if you are evolving and giving people what they want, then you will make share or make the demand rise. Taking share is a concept that does not include innovation and evolution in our products and services, as it simply takes customers away from other competitors.

Since we are distilling our culture, we should understand what culture is not. This is what culture is not:

- A slogan or words in writing on a break room wall.

- A fully funded organization that has not been tested by fire. Culture takes time to grow. Remember your high school labs where you "grew" culture? Different definition, but you get the point.

- Your business plan.

- An aspiration or a dream to become without embodying it.

This is what culture is:
- Authentic.

- Character. As Ralph Waldo Emerson states in one of his essays, "A character is like an acrostic or Alexandrian stanza—read it forward, backward, or across, it still spells the same thing."

- People and language.

- Created with time and struggle.

- The way you treat people you think don't matter.

- The key to a sustainable and profitable organization.

- A "feel." Your customers will see and feel it from a million miles away. That feel is the result of genuine connection between your organization, its employees, and customers.

Even if your customers do not really like your product or service, they may still use it if they have to, but I have never wanted to build a "have to" company. I have always wanted to build a "want to" company. A "want to" company is one where your customers want your product or service and choose to do business with you because of the experience.

If your customers "want to," then you build brand loyalty and protect your organization. If you build a "want to" company, you will need culture, and to have culture, your story had better be true. When it's true, it's like the DNA of your body—someone may be able to clone you, but you will always be the true version, the parent version, with time on your side. And time is the key ingredient in any recipe. Every recipe in the world has one thing in common: time. The time it takes to cook or bake is unique to that recipe, culture, and even environmental conditions like altitude. It takes time to distill a culture.

I had also noticed a statement being repeated by our employees and every one of our communities. As I met with leaders and discussed problems and opportunities, I would keep hearing "how we did it there." Everyone who worked in our communities had worked somewhere else to start, with the exception of young employees who were at their first job. Those with prior experience would bring that experience to our communities and want to apply it with the statement "how we did it there." Since I had started the company because I aspired to enhance quality and do things differently, I was not OK with doing things "how we did it there." I wanted to clearly define "how we do it *here*." How we do it here would be our operating platform, and it would turn out to be the most effective system we ever developed.

We built a framework around why we work here, what we do here, what we value here, how we communicate here, how we work here, and where we are going from here. Here is what we came up with:

WHY WE WORK HERE:

At The Springs Living, we strive to create warm, comfortable communities that enhance the lives of our residents. Our goal is to help them live well with grace and dignity.

- We have chosen to work in a The Springs Living community because it fulfills more than our need to make a living. It fulfills our desire to serve others.
- We believe that each of us is an important part of something bigger than ourselves.
- We strive to be the best place for the best people to work.

WHAT WE DO HERE:

- At The Springs Living, our primary goal is to serve seniors and their families.
- We are passionate about doing the right thing.
- We carry the responsibility of helping residents write yet another very important chapter in their life.
- We provide exceptional service, seeking every opportunity to impress on each person we encounter how important they are to us.
- We do the chores so families and friends can focus on relationships.

WHY WE VALUE HERE:

- We value our integrity and do not tolerate ethical lapses.
- We recognize that every outcome at The Springs Living is a direct reflection on our organization and us individually.
- We value the cultural and spiritual traditions of our residents and each other. Our differences make us stronger.
- We recognize that excellent attendance contributes to the quality of life for our residents and the success of the company.
- We value work ethic and commitment to quality.

HOW WE COMMUNICATE HERE:

We listen intently with open ears and minds seeking to understand.

We recognize that we are "on stage" anytime we are on property or representing the company.

We are always patient, kind, and gentle with others, saying "please" and "thank you."

We always say "hello" and greet residents and guests by name.

We speak truthfully and directly, while always mindful of the confidentiality and privacy of our residents and each other.

We are considerate of the feelings and sensitivities of others.

HOW WE WORK HERE:

- We always approach and respond to our residents, their families, guests, and co-workers with warmth, compassion, and respect.
- We recognize that problems are our biggest opportunity. We are in the business to help others solve problems.
- We yield to residents and guests in the halls and doorways.
- We are watchful for noticeable changes in our residents' conditions and communicate with them to our team.
- We complete our reresponsibilities on time so we do not leave work for others.
- We deal with every situation calmly.
- We are always ready to help each other and seek help from others when needed.
- We frequently make suggestions and offer ideas.
- We embrace change.
- We enjoy giving our residents an appropriate touch on the shoulder, a squeeze of the hand, or a hug.
- We are gentle with people and tenacious for quality.
- We are team players, loyal and supportive of each other.

What you might notice is that there are actually no values here. Each bullet point is actually a behavior. The problem with values is that they are difficult to measure. Not many people would argue with the value of compassion, but how do we really know if someone truly is compassionate? The same with the value of being generous. It turns out that the only way to measure a value like compassion is to look and observe if the person's behaviors are actually compassionate.

We measure values by someone's actions. Our list of "values" is actually a list of behaviors. The ways we measure behaviors are observations of behaviors, group interviews, etc.

People come with values; therefore, we needed to hire values that come inside of people. In selecting people, we distill for three areas: knowledge, skills, and abilities; values; and story.

Knowledge, skills, and abilities (KSA) are the three baseline requirements of any job. We distill for KSA by evaluations, a person's education, work history, and aptitudes for the job. Most organizations do this part really well. We have HR policies and procedures that generally perform this screening very well. Governmental agencies focus on this part of the distillation process.

Distilling for values, the next area, is a bit tricky, and I am not sure I have fully figured out how to do this well with 100 percent accuracy. Here is what I know. Values are indicated by behaviors. The problem with this during the interview process is that you have limited time. The best method I have found is to discuss each value and ask the interviewee to tell you how they have demonstrated that value. If they are true to the values you are looking for, they will be able to articulate behaviors that you will recognize. Involve one or two more people on your team to interview the person to get their opinions. Seasoned leaders who you know hold the values you are looking for will recognize others who also have those values. Consensus, while not 100 percent accurate, will increase your chance.

One of the ways we did this was to read a parable called "The Starfish Story" and then watch who really was moved by its simplicity. This helped us identify or distill who really wanted to work in service of others versus people who just needed money and could go down the street to a retail store or to work in a fast-food restaurant.

The Starfish Story

Adapted from "The Star Thrower," by Loren Eiseley (1907–1977)[7]

Once upon a time, there was a wise man who used to go to the ocean to do his writing. He had a habit of walking on the beach before he began his work. One day, as he was walking along the shore, he looked down the beach and saw a human figure moving like a dancer. He smiled to himself at the thought of someone who would dance to the day, and so, he walked faster to catch up.

As he got closer, he noticed that the figure was that of a young man and that what he was doing was not dancing at all. The young man was reaching down to the shore, picking up something, and very gently throwing it into the ocean.

As he got closer, he called out, "Good morning! What are you doing?" The young man paused, looked up, and replied, "Throwing starfish into the ocean."

"I must ask, then, why are you throwing starfish into the ocean?"

"The sun is up, and the tide is going out. If I don't throw them in, they'll die."

Upon hearing this, the wise man commented, "But, young man, do you not realize that there are miles and miles of beach, and there are starfish all along every mile? You can't possibly make a difference!"

The young man listened politely, then bent down, picked up another starfish, and threw it into the ocean, past the breaking waves and said,

"It made a difference for that one."

---

7   Loren Eiseley, "The Star Thrower," in *The Unexpected Universe* (New York: Harcourt, Brace & World, 1969), 120.

I always insisted on reading this aloud, pausing at inflection points to look around the room and see who was really engaged and listening and who was texting or not paying attention. You can get a strong indication by looking at someone's eyes as to whether they are a good fit. It is a powerful story and great to use to gauge someone's heart and emotional intelligence.

Another way we worked to gauge if potential employees shared our values was to show a video. In the early days, as an executive director I would hold what we called Springs Info Sessions— basically group meetings to answer questions about the job and gauge people's interests. I started bringing the DVD disc of my grandmother's life we had made for her end-of life celebration. Set to her favorite songs, pictures of her as a young girl, a young woman, married with children, and other life milestones slowly dissolved into the next like the CliffsNotes of a book. The ending of the video was powerful, which summed up a powerful woman. The first time I did this, I was not sure if it was a good idea. I simply wanted them to know why I did what I did. As I pressed stop on the DVD player and turned around, there was not a dry eye in the place, and I knew these would be people who would care well for our residents.

Measuring story is next. Your story is an important part of the process. Not just for the interviewer but for the interviewee. Listening to the connection of events is an important indicator of future success. Story helps get to someone's why, and someone's why is an indicator of what their attention and focus will be. As employers, when you can connect someone's why to your why, you can significantly increase the impact of story.

As I considered all this in developing our company, I called all our executive directors and managers to the office. We sat around the table, and I asked, "What are our values?" The next couple of hours rolled by like a couple of minutes. In that amount of time, we had managed to pen our purpose, our mission, and our plan. Further, we created five pages of behaviors under the titles "How we do it here," "How we communicate here," "How we treat each other here," and "Where we are going from here." We penned things like "We are tender with people and tenacious for quality." We said, "We yield to others in the hallways and always offer a warm greeting and say please and thank you." We also included, "We embrace change" as a cornerstone. It turns out embracing change and being able to pivot is a requirement for any organization that wants to change the world—and we wanted to change the world.

KEY TAKEAWAYS:

- Like all food recipes, culture needs time in order to get it right.

- When you make moonshine, you use process, heat and time to extract the exact recipe you desire—use this concept in selecting your employees, customers, and investors.

- Organizational culture cannot simply be copied or bought—it must originate from and reflect the authentic story, purpose and values of the organization's founders and leaders. Consultants can advise but not create a culture.

- Understanding the history behind an organization, its name, and its founders, even unflattering parts, builds self-awareness to guide values and culture establishment.

- Staff selection should attempt to assess and distill three ingredients—knowledge, skills, and abilities; values and associated behaviors; and personal story or purpose alignment.

CHAPTER 9

Organizational Culture Clarity

If you hire people just because they can do a job, they'll work for your money. But if you hire people who believe what you believe, they'll work for you with blood and sweat and tears.

—Simon Sinek

Growing up at Lehman Hot Springs, twenty miles from the nearest small town of 143 people and an hour and a half from the larger town, Pendleton, Oregon, with fifteen thousand people, gave me a sense that I was not really ever in the know. What went on outside the fields and forest of my home? People who came to swim or visit seemed worldly and sophisticated, and our family served them. I knew the outdoors, the animals, the dangers. Each time we would go to Pendleton, or on rare occasions, Portland, Oregon, I would observe and try to take in as much as possible, the way I would walk through the woods when hunting or gathering huckleberries or mushrooms. I knew that if I started out slow, observing every tree and movement around me, step by step, I would have a chance to see whatever was out there before it saw me. Naturally, I translated this woodsman skill to the big city and later to growing a business.

When I started my own company, The Springs Living, I did the same thing. I went slow, holding back, not focusing on growing, slowly working to understand our business and the market, and waiting patiently for the right next opportunity. As of the writing of this book, I have been in business twenty-seven years, and we only have twenty communities. Seemingly small in number, yet the approach, like walking through the Blue Mountains, has yielded a fair knowledge of my surroundings and twenty high-quality communities that we and our partners own.

One of the things I have observed in growing our business was that we never quite seemed to fit into the "business box." What I mean is that almost every business book I read and every consultant I would talk to preached the importance of having a hierarchical organizational structure and doing more to control the process and outcomes. Yet we focused first on relationships. Our small company wanted to grow up to be a real company someday, and from everything I could tell, a real company needed to have an organizational structure like a pyramid. It was a world in which I was supposed to sit on the top as we climbed steadily higher, with everyone under me and our executives. Exalted in my corner office like a king on a throne, I could survey the vast landscape of American capitalism while rising higher and higher as the company grew. After all, this is the American dream, right? It's what I remember that all my books on organizational development from business classes in college taught.

A reader, I have bought so many books over the years that even now my home office is overflowing with books offering new ideas on how to run and grow my business. Like in this one, authors like me would draw diagrams of vertical and horizontal organizational structures with the CEO at the top. One structure that I did seem to identify with was the pinwheel, which is used a lot in education. The pinwheel offered more of an organic structure of hubs and spokes. Yet, when asked by bankers, investors, or management teams how we were organized, we would stuff everyone into the hierarchical organizational structure that their business culture understands. Every time I did this, I felt like a fish out of water. It was like I was checking the box of what you are supposed to do to be a real business.

Over the years, I cannot tell you how many organizational structures we had. It seemed we revised and morphed them every few months, creating position names to make people feel good or like they were moving up the ladder. Everyone wants to move up the ladder, but I could never quite understand why. Eventually you get to the roof, and that is just not a great place to be, especially in a storm. Yet we complied.

Early on, in preparation for a company management meeting, I took my PowerPoint pyramid and rotated it 180 degrees so that the point was inverted. On paper it looked unstable with the base in the air in a precarious balancing act. On the top of that base, I put the words "residents and their families," our customers. Directly under that I put the words "direct care staff," our employees. Pausing, I looked back and thought I had just drawn a point of view that finally made sense to me. After all, in a business of caring and supporting others 24-7, 365 days a year, our success was 100 percent in the interaction between our customers and the frontline staff. It seemed to make sense.

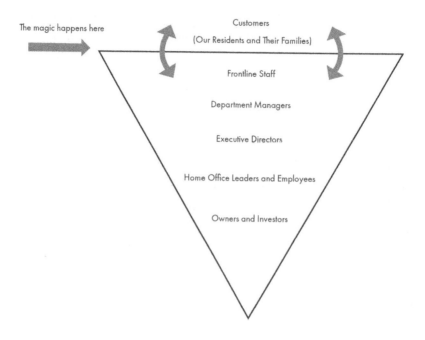

The magic happens here

Customers
(Our Residents and Their Families)

Frontline Staff

Department Managers

Executive Directors

Home Office Leaders and Employees

Owners and Investors

At the bottom of the upside-down pyramid, I put myself. Above me I put my team. Above them was middle management and then executive directors and supervisors. In those days we didn't have regional managers or any vice presidents, titles that mark the entrance of organizations into the bureaucratic and political quagmire. All I know is that this made sense and felt natural. This organizational structure looked more like a root system of a large tree, with the taproot going deep into the ground to give what is seen above the earth stability. It also reminded me of what I imagined lay below the bubbling hot springs at Lehman—a fissure of hot water coming from the earth's core rising to the surface and connecting with the air in many places. Either way, it was a natural organizational structure that made sense to me.

But it didn't make sense to many people outside our close-knit team. It wasn't in any textbook I had ever seen, nor was it taught by any of the capable management consultants we hired over the years to help our fledgling organization grow and get better. Behind closed doors and in our early management training we talked about it, but once we connected with the outside world of business professionals, we would translate it into the typical hierarchical organizational structure to show our power structure. It was as if those traditional organizational structures were like puppeteers. The puppet master was at the top with many strings connected to manipulate the frontline puppets for the customer. This made no sense to me. Not only was I not smart enough to be a puppet master, micromanaging every detail, but I couldn't see how in a 24-7, 365-day-a-year business I could stay on top of everything.

The hierarchical organizational structure just didn't fit us. Like a thousand-piece puzzle missing key pieces, I was stuck and for the life of me could not figure out why I was so uncomfortable with the traditional organizational structure. I felt the same way as a student in our American educational system that places people into boxes and favors a certain type of learner. My learning ability is not mainstream, and neither is my business approach. Why does every business have to fit into one box or, in this instance, a triangle? Yet we would give our bankers the piece of paper that showed something they could understand.

All that changed when I met psychologist Bill Schneider.

I opened the book that had just arrived from Amazon. The cover seemed benign and to the point. *Lead Right for Your Company's Type*, Schneider called it. As I made it through the chapters, I felt as if I had finally connected with someone who knew our company. His book was so impactful, because someone was finally validating my experience and offering guidance from that perspective, that I got on a plane and flew to Colorado to meet him.

The Schneider organizational system explained that organizations had different customer promises, cultures, and leadership approaches. Customer promise defined the enterprise type. He hypothesized, then proved with years of research, that there are four types of enterprises: Predictable/Dependable, Customized, Best-in-Class, and Enrichment. Each of the four enterprises has its own appropriate culture and leadership approach. Each enterprise is a unique combination of what it pays attention to and how it makes decisions. Predictable/Dependable and Customized primarily attend to "Actuality" matters (concrete, tangible reality). Best-in-Class and Enrichment primarily attend to "Possibility" matters (imagined alternatives, what might occur in the future). Predictable/Dependable and Best-in-Class decide by "Impersonal" means (fact/data based, objective). Customized and Enrichment decide by "Personal" means (judgment intensive, subjective).

Bill's research explains the successes of The Springs Living.

Our customer promise is Enrichment. We believed in creativity, stewardship, and values that we lived and breathed. Almost any Enrichment enterprise is grassroots; it springs from goodwill, values, and beliefs and is rooted in people's possibilities. Change goes with the territory, with no limits, no end points, and always more to be done.

Bill espoused four cultures: Collaboration, Control, Competence, and Cultivation. Bill proposes that it's your "customer promise" that determines your organizational culture and your leadership approach. Each culture is unique and needs a unique leadership approach to make it effective. The culture that aligns with our Enrichment customer promise is a Cultivation culture.

In a Cultivation culture, Schneider says organizations that serve an aspirational purpose need a clear identity and direction, and they even need permission to be authentic and not get framed into the one-size-fits-all box. Life is messy. In a Cultivation culture, you have to think differently. You have to change the paradigm just a little to be able to be OK with the mess. Emotions and feelings are a big part of how we deliver on our promises, and that can just be too messy for control-oriented leaders. You want an enrichment enterprise leader to understand this and have experience growing relationships, not scaling functional processes. However, functional processes are important and must be part of the mix; you want your leadership to see functional processes as a support, not as your primary aim. As in any organization and in any culture, leadership is the biggest predictor of quality and success. I have seen many years of means and methods designed to be the magic bullet to an organization's success, but in my experience empowering the right leaders is the number one key to fulfilling your promise to your customers. But it's not just about the right leaders. It's about the right leaders at the right time in your organization's development.

Like human development, organizations need different instruction and leadership for different life stages. A middle school teacher is unique and able to instill just the right amount of knowledge for the age of the child. But how they do this is the key. A very technical teacher in a four-hundred-level college class would most likely not be the right leader of this middle school class filled with budding humans overflowing with new surges of hormones. Therefore, whom you select as leaders is your number one way to ensure that you fulfill your organization's customer promise.

Enrichment Enterprises, Bill's definition for cultures of Cultivation, are judgment-based organizations because they promise to take care of people. These cultures are human-focused and messy. Emotions matter in our culture, but so does fulfilling business promises. To be successful you must carefully build functional process, and that takes judgment, and judgment takes leadership.

CHAPTER 10

Leading in a Culture of Promise

Never doubt that a small group of thought-ful, concerned citizens can change the world. Indeed, it is the only thing that ever has.

–Margaret Mead

At Lehman Hot Springs, the narrow canyon gains in elevation as you follow it south from the main attraction, the pools. Guarded by a stand of old-growth ponderosa pines, the area no longer than the length of a city block is where fifty hot springs bubble out of the ground, forming a hot stream and flowing into inviting swimming and soaking pools. Their chemical makeup is as unique as a human's DNA. These springs flow true north, downhill. First one, located at the highest point, is joined by another and another as the volume of water builds from a trickle into a stream to eventually be captured like fish in a net, where it is settled and cooled and then metered out into the pools where guests soak to heal and relax in the rich mineral waters. The springs gather around the main channel that funnels that liquid gold to fill the pools. An array of soaking and swimming pools is enclosed by the decorative fencing like the curtains of a great stage, hiding the busy production of the springs behind. In the morning, the steam rises off of the pools floating upward into the deep-blue mountain sky, rising and falling like the applause at a curtain call. When swimming in the pools, the audience of visitors does not see behind the curtain to the source, where nature has choreographed the chaotic but beautiful production that fills the pools and creates the visitors' experience. Behind the scene and out of sight of the customer, lessons can be learned.

Leaders Use Story

It all starts at the source. People are drawn to this place because of the springs, which produces a high quality and sufficient quantity of hot mineral water. Surrounded by an authentic story that informs and entertains. An organization's story, like its leaders, is like a window to the soul of that organization. Our stories connect us to all our stakeholders in a powerful and clear way. Our customers can learn who we are and what and how we meet their needs through our story. Leaders are drawn to the culture as it informs them if the organization is a good match for them, and our investors can discover key insights for their investment decisions. Story is clarity, and clarity is speed. I have worked with hundreds of managers in my career, and only a handful of true leaders come to mind, each of them effective in the connection of their personal story to the organization they become a part of. Each of them spotlighted by the team they serve.

When you first arrive at Lehman Hot Springs and enter through the front doors of the lodge, your gaze is immediately drawn away from the lodge itself out toward the water. Beyond the beautiful and enticing pools is a hidden door. Know the right place to push and it opens to reveal their source. What customers first see is not the containers of concrete and tile that hold the water, which on their own are cold, hard, and uninviting. Their gaze is drawn to the warmth inside and the steam rising from the surface. Likewise, our customers' experience with our organizations is a direct reflection of the leadership inside, exactly like the soothing and healing water in the pools. Each of us is a human vessel that unless filled with a purpose, a cause, or a why cannot reach our full potential for success. Leadership techniques, positional authority, and desire to be a leader are not enough alone to create a great organization. Story connects us to others, and having a purpose is what drives me every day to get up and get moving.

But the story is not just the good stories—it's equally the failures in our story that determine our leadership quality. Leadership is about connecting the dots, or in this story the hot springs, in our lives. If you didn't grow up at a hot spring resort, which likely you did not, it doesn't matter. What matters is your story. Knowing who you are and what you want today, even if that is still evolving, is the secret of your story. I hear people say that they don't know what they want out of life and so they feel paralyzed. For me, knowing that I didn't know was a great place to start. I learned to explore, take a chance, and just move in a direction. When you embrace yourself, your skills but also your imperfections and failures, you allow your story to draw you toward opportunity, just like my grandma's magnets drew each other when the positive end was turned toward the negative end. Both the successes and failures of our life are our story, and both equally connect us to our source and our future.

Leaders Are Strong Enough to Be Authentic

Being authentic means being willing to be vulnerable, to let ego go so that you can get to the root of what it takes to fulfill your promises. To be authentic means you need to 'shine. To 'shine you need to use failure to your advantage. I didn't say it's a leader's job to "shine," like they are in the spotlight, all about themselves. I said it's their job to *'shine.*

> *'Shine*
> *The apostrophe indicates the omission of letters. Our task is to distill the meaning of the apostrophe in our lives and in our work. To seek out and embrace the undiscovered and messy parts so that we can succeed and leave our part of the world better. Society tells us we need to only put our best self forward, hiding our flaws. I think not, because only when we accept and embrace our whole story can we 'shine.*
>
> *—Me*

My grandfather's story about making moonshine is an example of how story can be used to communicate and lead. For years my grandma was embarrassed by the roots of our past. She did not want to embrace the messy parts of our family's story. As a young leader, I used to feel the same way about my personal story. Without a college degree, failing at jobs and business, I felt that to be successful I had to hide my failures and put forward an image of invincibility and success. That was not authentic. I started my career during the 1980s when business was all about image. *Dress for Success* was a best-selling book. It would take many years for me to develop the ability to embrace my whole story.

For me, that apostrophe was covering up what I considered my failures and the dark side of my history. *Moon* was the word hidden in my story—put together with the word *shine*, it makes *moonshine*. That is as authentic as my grandfather's recipe. Illegal at the time, my grandfather's business made a product that was desired by many of the successful and powerful no matter how unsavory in its association and production. For me the story of moonshine was about more than our family's story. Its discovery gave me the courage I needed to embrace my whole story, including my many personal failures.

Our family lost our source, Lehman Hot Springs, in 1988 through bankruptcy due to bad market conditions during the Savings and Loan Crisis but also due to some poor decisions that put debt on the property. I had no idea how important that experience would be for me in the future as I guided our company through a future economic crisis. I cannot tell you the devastating impact that had on me and our entire family. The years that followed were unbearable, dark, and hopeless. But in that dark place I found the seeds for the future. Buried deep in the ground like the seed of a pine after a forest fire, that seed started to grow. Slowly I came to realize that I could turn the loss into success. I had no other choice but to look at it that way.

When I started The Springs Living, Lehman Hot Springs had not been owned by our family for ten years. That absence fueled my desire and the perspective that while a physical place had been ripped from my life, I still carried the most important parts of it with me—the ideas, values, and principles I had learned there. I found peace with the loss, an inner place where I would no longer let excuses hinder me. No one was coming to save me. The self-pity, excuses, self-doubt, and listening to others more than myself, while a temporary escape, were preventing me from moving forward. I learned that my failures could produce the most powerful opportunities. Many of us, if not all of us, have had dark days when we were lost. I did not start to see success until I realized that it was my whole experience, all of me, that was important. I have found the most effective leadership is much like this natural place—authentic.

Each hot spring is unique; so must leaders of organizations be authentic. If you walked along the hot creek and looked closely at each spring bubbling out of the ground, you would see that none is the same. They each have unique features, rocks, and shapes, but what flows out of them, the hot healing water, is the same. Like leaders in an organization should share a common set of values and core beliefs in what they are doing, these springs flow from the same deep source. Being authentic means that you embrace your whole story, your true story. Being authentic is about being trustworthy and comfortable in your own skin. The most effective leaders know how to embrace their whole story no matter how vulnerable. The best leaders do not hide behind a veil of positional power or pedigree. I don't believe we can become great leaders unless we are trustworthy, and that means trusting ourselves even after we have failed.

Embracing this truth demystified the failure for me. The mental barriers that limited me and prevented me from fulfilling my aspirational promises to myself and my family dissolved when I embraced my whole story to trust in providence and a lot of hard work.

Shared Values Attract Leaders

Lehman has more than fifty individual springs. The volume of water from just one of those springs is not enough to fill the pools and warm the swimmers. It takes all fifty springs to fill the pool. People are drawn to the bubbling springs, the steaming pools, and the towering pines at Lehman because it is real. People want to be there; I want to be there. It is not man made, except for the construction of the pools to harness that natural opportunity. We construct our organizational structures in a similar manner, built to take advantage of an opportunity or solve a problem or fill a need. But if you want to really make a difference, you need to attract people who share those values to the cause. Fill your pool with your own hot spring water that comes from deep within you, and others will join. You must create a place you want to be yourself before others will want to join you. We don't want to follow a position or even a person but rather be a part of a common purpose that is articulated through a story. The source of that purpose comes from deep inside you, your values, your knowledge, your skills and abilities but also your journey.

Leaders attract other leaders with similar values. We must build teams of like-minded individuals, albeit with different and complementary KSAs, who agree on the promise, vision, and goals of the organization. Attracting leaders is about being authentic and committing to your unique place in life and sharing common values and vision. The hot springs at Lehman grow in number as they descend down the canyon toward the soaking pools; just like as organizations grow, they need to attract like-minded leadership.

Leaders understand human nature. While pay, reputation, and values will initially attract the leadership to an organization, leaders will not stay there if the organization is not structured to benefit those leaders in their personal lives. "A rising tide lifts all boats" is a great way of saying that leaders must understand they need to create organizational environments where everyone can thrive.

Leaders Keep the Springs Clean

Great leaders deal with problems promptly. This means sometimes we have to do hard things like ask people to leave our organization even if they are invested in its story. Leaders do hard things not because they are cruel or enjoy causing pain but because they know if they don't deal with the problem now, they will have to deal with it when it grows bigger. And when problems grow big, it puts not only the organization at risk but the leader themselves. Problems grow and never magically disappear on their own. They can fester and brew for years before you finally incur their wrath. That's what leaders do—resolve problems. Resolving problems promptly is respectful, professional, and shows that you care—and besides, it's just smart. Fulfilling aspirational promises can only be done by solving problems, and that is what we do when we keep our hot springs clean.

As we walk through the secret door in the fence at the back of the pools, we look up to see a picture of the pure water bubbling out of the ground, clear, clean, and full of energy. I imagine this is similar to almost anyone who takes a job in an organization of their own free will. Never have I hired anyone who wanted to screw up, get fired, get frustrated, or quit when they started. Yet it happens every day. Like the hot water bubbling from the springs, people take positions in organizations with expectations that are pure and full of energy, just like the water. At the hot springs, although the water is pure and the heat intense, when it mixes with sunlight, air, and other organisms, it causes a natural process of growth. Moss and algae of all shapes and sizes appear in no time. Then, in this natural habitat, bugs, snakes, or other creatures find their way into the scalding waters, only to succumb to its intense heat. All these natural contaminants grow larger, breaking off and flowing into the pristine pools where the customers swim. Likewise, in any organization human relationships start off with pure and good intent. Yet contaminants grow in the form of miscommunication, politics, greed, and jealousy that pollute relationships and the work environment. If left to grow, they will break off and flow out into your employees' and customers' experiences, causing damage to your culture and brand. The answer is to keep the springs clean and your culture true to its origin: crystal clear.

At Lehman, when we clean the pools, we also clean the springs, because if you just clean the pools, it won't be long until the algae will break off at the source and cause the pools to get murky and dirty, making it a waste of time to even clean the pools. When you take care of your culture, you take care of your customers' experience. The first step we take in cleaning the springs is to isolate the pools from the hot springs by closing a valve and diverting the water out into a bypass that lets it harmlessly flow into the creek on the other side of the pools. It is important when cleaning your relational and cultural springs in the organization to do the same things and deal with personnel and management problems out of the view of your customers. Cleaning the springs takes place on a routine basis at Lehman Hot Springs. It also takes place every day at The Springs Living. We clean our cultural springs by the way we focus on keeping our promises and our organizational relationships by conducting one-on-ones, daily jump-start meetings for departments, or monthly management meetings for teams.

Cleaning the springs is not complicated, but when you are in the middle of it, the water turns an awful color as particulates and debris mix and break down and make the springs that just a moment before looked pure now look like swamp water. When you're doing it, sometimes it seems as if the water will never be clear again. Yet give it a little time, and the flow of pure water pushes the contaminants down the springs and out the diversion pipe harmlessly into the waiting stream, and once again you have water that is inviting. You get the point. In a culture of promise, you protect your culture by dealing with problems in a timely manner.

It is the same for your organization. It is tempting not to deal with HR issues, miscommunication, or problems because you are busy and it's not that bad. Yet doing so is a risk to your reputation, which is a risk to your culture. Just as in accounting, where you balance debits and credits, you want to keep the relationship accounts balanced and to do so in a way that is direct, timely, and respectful. Leaders know they must deal with small problems before they become big ones. Matching leaders to the organizational culture is the key. Put the wrong style of leader in a culture of promise, and you will soon find yourself swimming in a dirty pool.

Finding the Best Leaders for Your Culture

Cultures of Promise are defined by their promise, and that promise determines the leadership makeup that organization needs. I am going to touch on this point only briefly because my understanding and work on this subject is just in its infancy. But if I had realized this years ago, our organization would be years ahead of where we are now. Not every leader should lead a culture where the promise is to take care of others. Some cultures promise to produce widgets in factories, some promise to discover the next energy technology, and others yet promise to be experts and help you in tasks like building a house. The key is to match leadership styles with the organizational culture.

I had briefly worked as a consultant for a man who was in the real estate business. This person was very financially successful and drove a hard bargain; he also drove his people hard. I experienced some of that hardness in a closed-door meeting and witnessed a barrage of abuse. Fortunately it was not directed at me, but never the less I vowed to never treat anyone like that. The verbal abuse was a demonstration of abusive power, which is what some people use to control others.

A few years later, this person went into senior housing, building a business and several communities. At this time I had not started my own business, but that experience became one of the motivators for me starting The Springs Living just a few years later. No way was I going to let a person who treated people so poorly take care of my grandmother or anyone I cared about. That was the first time I realized that different cultures need different leadership styles. Much has been written on this subject, and taking time to dig into matching the right leadership style for your organization will be well worth its time investment. One sure way to see if someone is capable of leading in a culture of promise is to watch how a person treats people to whom they don't have to be nice. I am not talking about the occasional office blowup, although that's never a best practice. I am guilty of letting my passion and emotions get away from me from time to time. I am speaking about how leaders treat the server at the restaurant, the custodian at the stadium, or the entry-level employee at the company. Finding leaders who don't just believe in your organization's values but who *are* your organizational values makes all the difference.

Leaders Must Do One Thing

Leaders in a culture of promise must be empowered to use judgment to do one thing: the right thing. While policies and procedures in your organization are important, you can never let them overrule the judgment of your leaders in the moment. That is why you hire values. If you have consistent values, then you can trust the judgment of your leaders. When we hire someone, we go to great lengths to distill for values. If we hire that person, we feel they have demonstrated that they share our organizational values and therefore have judgment. We empower those leaders to use those values to make decisions to do the right thing. What is the right thing? It's quality. What is quality?

We define it as follows:

- Quality of relationships

- Quality of the work

- Quality of you

The quality of relationships is perhaps the most important element of your business. Especially in business that takes care of others, if you have a trusting relationship with your customers and your employees and even your capital partners, you can overcome almost any obstacle. The second element of quality is the actual work. Customers pay us to be good and to execute well on our promises. Leaders must be continually improving the quality of their product and its delivery. However, no matter how good you are, you will fail at times, and during those failures your fail-safe is your relationship.

Underlying all this is the quality of you. This means leaders must make sure each of the people they lead, including themselves, has what they need and are building quality in their life. When you care about each person and want the best for them, it always works out best for you. The worst thing to do is try to keep people in your organization if they really want to be somewhere else. Working with your team to develop career development plans, even if that takes them away from you, is always a good idea. When people know you care and can see that demonstrated, not just talked about, they feel safe and are more likely to do well in their jobs. When there is trust between a leader and those they are responsible for supporting, it's amazing what you can accomplish. This means you will be vulnerable to people taking advantage of you and the company. No worries—anyone who will take advantage of you is not someone you want in your organization. When you hold the point of view that if something is not good for you, it cannot be good for others, and vice versa, you create safe environments. The quality of *you* is exactly why we choose to define our purpose as "to help our residents, their families, and each other live life to its fullest." This perspective is a great way to continually clean your springs.

Positional Power versus Leadership Power

Leaders find ways to connect to people in a way that people "want to" instead of "have to." It's not an either/or scenario, though. Just as nothing is black or white, you must use judgment based on the scenario. Leaders know when to use "have to" and not abuse it. The goal would be to lead by inspiring and directing folks to *want to* at least 99 percent of the time. While it is ideal to create a 100 percent "want to," I just haven't found that possible with every person you are responsible to lead.

Leaders Are Guardians of the Galaxy

Earlier, I used the analogy of the guardians of the galaxy. This extends to leadership. The ecosystem at the hot springs is fragile. As its steward, our role is to nurture and protect them so they can nourish those who are here now and those who will follow. Leadership protects these natural resources, and just like we protect the springs, we protect the natural environment of each of our organizations. It's a leader's job to guard the environment, our galaxy.

Soaking in the warm waters makes you feel better, lighter, and able to move as if you were a much younger person. In the pools silica coats your skin, softening it and making you feel as if you are covered in silk. The lithium absorbs, slowly giving you a sense of deep relaxation, safety, and warmth. This is metaphorically what we provide to our residents and their families at The Springs Living. Just like you can feel the warmth when you soak in the pools, you can also feel this when you walk into our communities. Don't ask me how, but we often have people tell us that you can feel the care, love, and compassion when they walk in our doors. There is a thickness in the air that is warm, authentic, and people can feel that we are genuine in our aspirational promise to create great environments to live in. The feeling cultivates our relationships. Allowing and protecting the environment, to use another metaphor, is like a farmer cultivating their soil to grow crops; we cultivate our environment to grow relationships. Our leaders are farmers, protecting the environment, because when you create environments and fill them with people aligned in a common aim, you cannot stop the quality from growing.

Leaders Have Grit

In 1994, on top of the Peachtree Hotel in Atlanta, I had discovered that this place offered a model for how to create a senior housing and care organization and how to build each community. Since then, I had held true to the principle of the source, the sacred water, as the metaphor that we had to fill our buildings with people who had values and care to serve the residents. Like for hundreds of years visitors came to the waters of Lehman Hot Springs, older adults needing support in their lives would come to our communities because of the people who cared and supported them. I have always known our success was about one thing, our people—more specifically, about the quality of love, compassion, and competence those people provide our customers.

But when I started The Springs Living, all I had was a metaphor and a memory.

In 1988, the wind of adversity during the great FDIC/Savings and Loan Crisis swept Lehman Hot Springs from us. That event devastated our entire family, and the gray clouds of failure and financial instability rolled in like a mountain storm. We would survive that storm to see the next economic storm called the Great Financial Crisis, sweep our family treasure back to me. On July 19, 2012, I repurchased Lehman Hot Springs after the then owner defaulted on his loan, and I vowed to never have debt against it again. Owning Lehman once again has allowed us to care for this land the way it deserves, renovating and restoring the ancient place. We now bring our leadership teams to learn its secrets and the lessons it has to teach us. Our goal is to surround our residents and their families with support, care, and professional services just like the soothing waters of Lehman Hot Springs envelope you when you soak in their waters. We want to make them feel like they make our residents feel—warm, comfortable, safer, and better. This ancient and sacred place now cares for the people who care for all the grandparents we serve.

Lehman Hot Springs in the 1960s, a popular gathering place for friends and families.

While I always carried the idea of Lehman Hot Springs in my heart, to have it back physically today means the world to me. It feels like the completion of a circle or the fulfillment of a destiny where I can share its beauty and its lessons. For me, leadership boils down to the person, and each person, each leader, must be authentic, vulnerable, humble, confident, competent, and trustworthy. Leadership is about supporting people to achieve outcomes based on shared vision, values, and beliefs. Leadership is also the ability to embrace your story and use that personal story, whether tragic or triumphant, to add energy, determination, and passion to everyday life. It is all about leadership, because unless you can grow your leadership, you cannot grow your organization in a culture of promise.

KEY TAKEAWAYS:

- Leaders must be vulnerable and authentic to build trust. Presenting an image of perfection hinders this.

- Problems left unchecked erode culture like debris contaminating pure water from a spring. Timely resolution maintains cultural clarity and quality. Contaminates include lack of communication, ego, feelings of safety among teams, just to name a few.

- Not all leaders fit all cultures. Care cultures need leaders focused on relationship quality, as well as metrics and status.

- Judicious empowerment of frontline staff to do one thing, the right thing, based on shared values is more effective than rigid policy adherence.

- Doing one thing, the right thing, means focusing on quality.

- Quality is defined as the quality of relationships, quality of the work we perform for our customers, and quality of life for every person that works in the organization which we call the quality of you.

CHAPTER 11

Growing a Culture of Promise

The Quality Growth Curve

I never dreamed about success. I worked for it.

—Estee Lauder

It was two in the morning, and the bartender had just made last call at the Wardman Park Marriott, in the Washington, DC, lobby bar where the National Investment Center (NIC) was holding its annual conference, the gathering place of all the public and private institutional investors in senior housing and care. Bill F. Lasky, the CEO of Alterra Senior Living, sat sipping his cocktail and enjoying a moment of triumph. He had just closed a multimillion-dollar deal to create a sizable company and sat spread out on the chaise like a prince entertaining his subjects. I sat listening as he told a handful of the last-call cohorts of his conquest. His confidence was as intoxicating as his final gin and tonic. His company had seen skyrocketing growth in the last few years. *The company ran fewer than twenty facilities in 1995, but by the next year it operated sixty-two residences in nine states, and this deal made them even bigger.* This was roughly about the year 2000 … and by 2005 Alterra would cease to exist.

The year Sunwest Senior Living closed its doors, they were up to over three hundred buildings and growing at a pace of one new building a week. Within a few years, this CEO would be wearing an orange jumpsuit with plenty of time to consider how he might have grown his company differently. Even the well-respected industry icon Paul Klaassen, famous for repeating the statement "There is no mission without margin," saw his venerable company, Sunrise Senior Living, file for bankruptcy and reorganize, inflicting damage to its quality and reputation.

In all these examples, companies prioritized growth over quality. Why did this happen, where did they go wrong, and what lessons can we glean? Sure, this was a tragedy for the investors, but how much more for the people who lived there, some of whom may have received substandard service and care? And what about the employees and the instability these difficulties brought forth in their lives?

Two companies are now the ghosts that wander the halls of the large national industry conferences where their CEOs once held court and commanded their legions of analysts and dealmakers. Ghosts in the sense that their presence can still be felt. They linger in the shadows, offering us lessons and guidance if we embrace them or a haunting reminder of the loss we can expect if we repeat the past. Sunrise Senior Living has emerged under new leadership to regain its stature as leader in senior housing and care. But these ghosts are not just limited to "for-profit" companies. The fact that organizations, good organizations with caring folks, outgrow their quality comes in many shapes and sizes. Let's

can use the 3D Vision table to explore your organizational
stry limiters, as discussed in chapter 6.

e 3D Vision imiters	Customers	Employees	Capital Partners
Move	Q: What limits customers from moving into senior housing? Possible answers: Affordability, reputation/quality of the facility, reputation/quality of the industry, competition from the home, the facility value proposition.	Q: What limits employees from working in senior housing? Possible answers: Total compensation package, reputation of the facility, reputation of the industry, competition from other industries.	Q: What limits capital investments in senior housing? Possible answers: Risk-adjusted returns, reputation of the industry, lack of quality data about the industry, lack of understanding of the industry.
Stay	Q: What limits those who live in senior housing from not moving back to their homes or to another setting? Possible answers: Poor quality, no follow-through on promises, their ability to pay.	Q: What limits employees from staying on the job? Possible answers: Lack of upward mobility, employer's lack of understanding and investment into the workforce, physical and emotional difficulty of the work. Culture–feeling of belonging and connection.	Q: What causes investors to leave senior housing investments? Possible answers: Inconsistency in return results, losses, quality risks, loss of trust, failure to communicate.
Thrive	Q: What limits customers from thriving in this chapter of life? Possible answers: Physical health, establishing meaningful relationships, organizational focus on making thriving a priority.	Q: What limits employees from thriving in their careers? Possible answers: Lack of career opportunities, lack of educational opportunities, lack of organization including appreciation for the jobs they do, lack of tools to help deal with the physical and emotional strain of aspirational promises.	Q: What limits capital from investing more into senior housing and care? Possible answers: A commitment to the social good that senior housing and long-term care provide society, insufficient operational capacity to achieve quality outcomes.

be honest—this is not just a for-profit problem. For example, "mission creep" is an issue in nonprofits—where good intentions expand beyond the vision, wise business and operating decisions, and purpose at hand until they are spread too thin.

For the executives of these companies who frequent these conferences and are entertained with expensive wines and gourmet food (of which I am one), it can be hard to stay focused on the reason why they are there. Far removed from the frontline worker caring for a frail adult—both the physical effort and the emotional and professional strain—it is easy to lose focus. Time after time, empire builders have gathered their armies of MBAs to assault the walls of senior housing and care in search of the rich treasures of disposable private-pay income and government spending only to be crushed by one simple foe: quality. All these companies had one thing in common—the uncontrolled pursuit of growth. Yet Chris Galvin's comment to me all those years ago that size doesn't matter if we can define and expand our limiters haunted my thoughts like a song you cannot get out of your head. Over and over the chorus played, "It's not about the size of the company, it's about the limiters. Your industry just doesn't understand its limiters. Find the limiters."

How Many Buildings Do You Have?

The most frequently asked questions by capital providers at conferences is this: "How many buildings do you have?" They don't ask about your quality or how happy your employees are. They want to know about real estate and growth. And for good reason, because the United States of America's economy is all about real estate and growth. We understand real estate, and efficient capital markets invest in real estate, which is the cheapest cost of capital for the sector. Even our individual American dream is all about real estate. *Yet this is not a real estate business but a business that has real estate.* So, if it's not about real estate, what is it about? Capital providers, please ask this question, "How is your quality?" before you ask how big our companies are. Different organizations deserve different costs of capital based on the consistency of their results and the quality they can deliver.

Finding the Limiters to Quality

The causes of failed organizations are likely several, but one of those was because they didn't define and understand their organizational limiters and then invest in the infrastructure to expand their capacity for addressing those limiters to carry their weight and allow the growth to proceed.

Limiters are defined as business systems and resources, including people and capital, that do not have the capacity to carry the load that growth provides. Let's compare it to electricity. If you need a bigger machine at your plant for making widgets, it is likely you need a bigger-capacity wire for the extra power needed to run the plant. If you install the machine but don't upgrade the power, you are likely to break your new equipment. Low-voltage warning lights need to be installed in organizations just like on equipment. Also, organizations, like electrical service, need to ensure that the conduit for power, people, systems, and capital is suited to carry the load. Installing a higher-capacity wire is the same as installing bigger business systems to run your business. This is such a simple concept and business 101 that many other business sectors have already discovered long ago.

Don't forget to install a circuit breaker that will protect your organization the way breakers protect equipment. I think this is one of the key mistakes we have made. When a company does well with

one, two, or ten buildings, it's tempti
add money (i.e., power) and grow to, s
electrical panel in your home, we have
installing a breaker box that warns the p
coming down the line and that the com
If you are not watching closely, that cu
organization just like it did in the com
countless others).

You need to engineer your busir
expand your limiters and grow, and in
know what the limiters are. Explore fo
have populated some possible answers l
clusions. This matrix is a working tool

You
and indu

Poss

Your organization can apply this simple thought process around determining what you believe the root causes are to the limiters to growth and quality. I have populated some possible root cause issues that could be a part of any organization. But filling this out with your leadership teams will be well worth the exercise.

Possible Root Causes to Limiters

3D Vision Root Causes to Quality	Customers	Employees	Investors/Owners
Move	*Lack of systems and discipline that allows overpromising by your teams. *In new buildings, moving people in too fast before your community is ready to serve them. *Not understanding that you are growing relationships, not renting apartments.	*Not having a system to distill the selection of your employees and so you hire people who don't have aligned values, KSA, and story. *Negative word of mouth about what this industry is like to work in.	*Lack of the right capital for the right stage of your organization. *Taking of giving short-term management contracts or signing leases that are short-term focused, meaning operator business plans lack sufficient capital to make long-term decisions.
Stay	*Ignoring small customer service and quality problems. *Regulatory overburden. *Not building systems focused on quality outcomes.	*A weak HR deparment. *Excessive worker compensation claims. *High turnover in leaders.	*Poor accounting systems and reporting regimes. *Not growing your systems to meet the needs of your partners. *Weak understanding of the organizational culture.
Thrive	*Not empowering your leaders to meet your customers' needs. *Not having an open culture where employees can say something when they see a problem.	*Not holding poor performers accountable because you are understaffed (this will run off even the good staff). *Not understanding the frontline worker and workforce instability. *When employees think that the organization cares more about the money than the customer.	*Overpromising returns up front and not hitting return targets. *Not providing capital that invests in organizational infrastructure.

Identifying limiters should work backward from the interaction between the frontline worker and your customer. In a business that is about family, feelings, and life itself, any organization is only as good as the interaction between the care worker and the resident or customer. Period. The business systems must work from that impact point of view. And when, not if, it encounters problems, that you run to fix the problem. Can you imagine if a city grew and grew and grew without ever having a fire marshal who oversaw building codes to keep new buildings from burning? You would never be able to hire enough firefighters to keep up. Senior housing and care needs more fire marshals, not more firefighters. We need to build our quality the way we build our buildings—so it won't be burned down.

All those years ago when Chris Galvin of Harrison Street asked me about how big I wanted to grow, I said, "Not big," but not because I wasn't a big thinker. I am a goal-oriented dreamer like the next person, and being financially motivated and caring are not mutually exclusive. I do not hold the view that poverty is purity nor that all greed is good. I think there is a balance, and it's up to each person to choose where they want to fall along the spectrum. Your customers, employees, and partners have a vote in your success so you may want to include them in that success.

So why did I tell Chris that I didn't want to be a big company? Today, if you frequent the large national conferences where capital providers and operators go to connect, why do you think capital providers compete for the regional operators? Simple—because these smaller companies constantly have the best-quality outcomes. It's not that I didn't want to grow. I just didn't want to sacrifice quality for scale or break my business promises, nor did I want to let my grandma down.

The reason capital providers are targeting regionals is that they offer the best quality. It's not a judgment as to the best business formula.

What they are saying is that they see the best results coming from regional companies with twenty to fifty buildings. Quality can exist in large organizations because the size is actually an advantage—so long as you are fulfilling your promise. I have always been baffled about why, when organizations grow, their quality declines. If you have more resources, should not your quality rise? Of course it should—anything less means you have outgrown your quality.

The Quality Growth Curve: The Theory

The quality growth curve is a theory that holds that the size of an organization is only relevant if it can produce adequately to meet or exceed the quality expectations for its stakeholders. This includes customers, employees, and capital providers as primary stakeholders. Of course, more stakeholders can impact your business, like vendors and regulators, but for the purpose of our discussion here, we are focusing only on what I define as primary stakeholders. *This theory keeps the focus on the frontline results as the primary indicator that an organization is building a structurally sound enterprise.*

Defining Quality to Expand Your Limiters

In a culture of promise, where you are judged on how well you fulfill your promise to care for others, quality is measured in three ways for each of our 3D stakeholders. Quality is the quality of relationships, the quality of the work, and the quality of you, or each individual person in your organization.

You can use the 3D matrix to explore the elements you think are important for quality, but if I had to offer one thing that you must demonstrate to all your stakeholders, especially the employees, it is that you truly care for the residents and don't just see them with a dollar sign on their forehead. No doubt every organization will say they care, but beware—people have good bullshit detectors (I know mine is finely tuned!). You can't just say you care; you must truly care. We know if you care, not by what you declare your values to be on your website, but by seeing the evidence of their existence through your actions.

Elements of Quality

The elements of quality in a culture of promise start with relationships. In our company we measure quality broadly as the quality of our relationships with our stakeholders, the quality of the work itself, and the quality of you, which means we strive for each person in our organization to have the opportunity to benefit. Think of the relationship of these three elements of quality as a circle, where you enter the quality circle at the word *relationships*, then circle clockwise to *work*, and then continuing to *you*, as depicted in the diagram. A culture of promise takes the temperature by monitoring each of these indicators on a continuous basis. This is a flow, a cycle, a natural process that will help you grow quality.

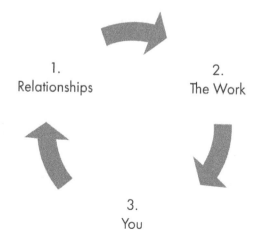

1.
Relationships

2.
The Work

3.
You

The relationship with your stakeholders is where it all starts. We start with relationships because when you have good relationships, you can recover from breaking your aspirational promises when things go wrong (and as we all know, they will—that is life itself). When you have quality relationships, even when you mess up the quality of work, and you will, you can actually build stronger customer connections. Admitting your own humanity is a vulnerable thing to do, but authentic persistence can build lasting bonds. We must not just strive to do better—we must actually do better.

Perfection in the work is impossible, so focusing on relationships will actually make the work better. Continuing clockwise in the diagram, you get to the quality of you. This is the part where you put on your seat belt, just like the flight attendants do, before you take off. And you put on your oxygen mask first, if needed, before putting it on others. This is where you invest in yourself, your employees, and your organization.

This concept is a natural cycle that considers each person you work with and each customer you serve. It also applies to your other stakeholders. You have to be sincere about your concern for everyone in your organization, and they have to not just know it but *feel* it. When your employees know you care about them, they know you care about the residents, and they will go to extraordinary lengths to make a difference in the residents' and their families' lives.

Charting Quality and Growth

The concept is simple: don't grow faster than your ability to fulfill your promises. The reality is far more complex, because it's actually not possible. Just like an aspirational promise is not possible to keep perfectly, neither is your ability not to outgrow your quality. In fact, at times you must outgrow your quality to reach your maximum potential. The key is to recognize when you are at the tipping point and correct. It is like lifting weights or exercising, when you are actually breaking down the body to get stronger and grow. To do that, you have to create an organizational environment in which you have systems and data to tell you where you are while also trusting the judgment of your leaders. Having good data is one thing, but having leaders with good judgment is the key. To play it too safe is to never reach your potential. Organizations that want to make a difference must take risks. Like in the story of the three little bears, our goal is to get our porridge just right.

Measuring your growth is easy. You can do it with the number of buildings, number of units, or people, or you can do it with your revenue growth. Measuring quality will be somewhat harder in a culture of promise because our promise is not a concrete promise. Taking care of someone requires that we look at some subjective inputs as well as the behaviors folks exhibit when we are fulfilling their promise, and that takes some judgment. Judgment can be applied in our individual organizations, but on an industry basis we need to rely on indicators that are common across the industry to measure quality with data. At the time I am writing this book, the industry, including its regulatory bodies, does not have agreement on what should be measured. An industry coalition of which I am currently participating is working to define which quality indicators should be measured. This effort is essential and should be applauded as a proactive step that shows the growing maturity of our sector and the leaders in it. We must reach agreements as an industry on these key quality indicators.

Since there is no current consensus as to what quality indicators should be measured as a standard like in other sectors like hospitals or hospitality, I will share my thoughts on these indicators. These thoughts are based on what I know today and have seen in my almost thirty-year career.

If we are going to chart quality and growth, we will need to pick indicators for both datasets: growth and quality.

Using the 3D Vision matrix, work to clearly understand the elements essential to fulfilling your promise.

Data points to plot your growth could be among these:

1. Number of buildings

2. Number of units

3. Top-line revenue

4. EBITDA or NOI CAGR (compound annual growth rate)

These are fairly straightforward, and you could look at just one to keep it simple or at some weighted measure of all of them. The indicators for growth can also be segmented by building, unit, per patient day, or other segmentation method.

The data points to measure quality are more complex, and this will no doubt take some refinement. Here are some possibilities arranged into categories:

1. Qualitative

   □ NPS (net promoter score).

   □ ENPS (employee net promoter score).

   □ Behavioral value indicators. This is a measure we are not ready to publish that will combine judgment-based analyses from qualified professionals that indicate the behaviors customers and employees exhibit when you are fulfilling your promise. We believe you can measure values only through observable behaviors.

2. Financial

- Occupancy. When you have quality, folks want to live with you. Besides the short-term occupancy challenges that are a natural cycle in communities, this is a simple and the biggest indicator of quality and value.

- Growth in net operating income or EBITDA. Ultimately your net income over a period of time (i.e., CAGR), like years, literally tells the bottom-line story of quality. My observation is that when you take care of people, your bottom line is stable and growing because your reputation creates demand, which allows you to grow your revenue.

- Aging report for payables. While confidential for every organization I know, this is one of the simplest ways to see how the financial infrastructure of an organization is operating. Keeping a promise is to pay bills on time. This is also an indicator of your professional reputation. Vendors have families who live in your communities, and if you don't pay your bills on time and keep your business promises, it will damage your reputation.

- Insurance indicators

  * Loss run.

  * Per-bed rate for PLGL (professional liability general liability).

3. Workforce

- Worker compensation claims and rates and trends.

▫ Employee retention rates. I like this more than turnover rates because in an industry where you have a lot of entry-level positions, you will always have a higher turnover of employees. In my opinion, if you have one-third of employees staying, one-third coming in, and one-third going out, that is likely the best that can be achieved. It takes new employees some time to see if they are cut out for the care profession. Tracking retention rates seems to be the best indicator of core dedicated employees.

▫ Leadership retention rates. This is a key indicator of culture and likely the most dependable data.

▫ Total compensation rates. Employees in today's workforce need more than just a paycheck. Programs like Workforce Stability provide eleven different benefits that will boost workforce support and success. All those cost money, and few of them are measured by politicians and bureaucrats. Companies and unions seem to be one-trick ponies around wages, many not even understanding our true workforce needs. Many good resources exist to inform people about these programs.

4. Healthcare

▫ Hospitalizations and emergency room visits.

▫ Falls with injury.

▫ Hospital readmission rates.

▫ Medicare spend per resident in communities.

▫ Number of medications per resident if you are operating a licensed community.

5. Other

- Manager or operator organizational infrastructure investment. We plan for capital expenditure in our buildings and real estate, so why would we not do the same thing for our infrastructure investment, especially if we are growing?

- Length of stay for residents.

Add more indicators if you want. This list is not meant to be exhaustive, just provocative. Organizations will improve quality just by embracing the quality growth curve (QGC) concept without even actually measuring quality. However, to plan to be a part of the future of the industry, you will need to measure and prove your value to the customers, to your capital, and to the healthcare industry. Translated, you will need to be able to empirically demonstrate your value to the customer, the healthcare system that supports them, and society. Prove that we will innovate to create the solutions and living environments that will enrich their lives.

Innovations create solutions and living environments that will enrich all stakeholders. In my experience, the best innovations rise up from the ground level, like a spring. They don't come from a bunch of executives sitting around a conference room table. Developing a culture that promotes ideas to get better and innovate in our own organizations and our industry will allow us to improve quality outcomes and change with our customer base. If you really think about it, each time we hire a brand-new employee, new to the industry, we change. They are from a younger generation and have new ideas. The same is true for our residents. In our communities, we have people from two generations. As new young people move into positions, we change and evolve. Setting up continuous improvement systems to change with our people and those we serve will keep our organizations relevant and sustainable.

The goal is to accurately measure the organization's ability to handle growth. This concept is important for managers, operators, and especially for capital partners. Simply by asking questions around this concept will help organizations focus on responsible growth. Normalizing a quality growth curve mentality in your organization changes your aiming point. Even if you cannot institute accurate charting of your growth and quality, making it a point of view will cause changes in your organization. It will empower leaders to focus on that point of magical interaction between your direct care staff and the residents and their family. Giving permission will set your team's entrepreneurial higher selves to focus on creating quality. All this focus is done in conjunction with keeping your eye on the bottom-line outcomes. You still need to hit your financial targets, but you may just find a way to do both. Unless you have quality and financial results, you cannot fulfill the good of being a culture of promise. Keeping aspirational promises and business promises is the core tenet of Cultures of Promise.

Charting your growth and quality may look something like the graph featured on page 181. This graph is for illustrative purposes, but it roughly matches the relationship my company has had growing quality.

Creating a Positive Quality Gap

The goal is to create more capacity for growth and still be able to keep your promises to your stakeholders. Anytime you create a positive gap, you have created the capacity to grow responsibility without sacrificing your promises. It stands therefore that when new companies start, they have a positive quality gap and they are ready to grow. They do well with one, two, and then three locations, and that provides them access to capital. That access will allow them to grow again, and that is when you have to be very careful. *Take it from someone who started with one building: your most dangerous point in your organization is when things are going very well and you decide to grow.* If you have done well initially, you will attract the capital to grow. Deciding how much to grow will be the key, and that is not an exact science. Your decisions at these organizational inflection points are what create your results and your brand reputation. Have no doubt, you will outgrow your quality. In fact, I encourage you to outgrow your quality—briefly.

Avoiding a Negative Quality Gap

When you outgrow your quality, you have created a negative quality gap (see the chart on page 181). When this happens, refocus and work to turn the quality gap positive. Putting the breaks on can be hard to do because growth can be addictive. Growth can create an altered perception of the reality of what is actually happening on the front lines. It is likely that you will know when you outgrow your quality, whether you can chart it or not. The question is will you correct your course when you become aware of a negative quality gap? It's at these growth inflection points that you need to focus on your reputation and seek to understand what is actually happening on the front lines. If you cannot keep up with fixing problems for your stakeholders that were created by your growth, you have just grown past your quality. All these can be seen in the numbers, but the right leadership can just tell and they are strong enough to do something about it. When retention of your key employees declines, worker compensation claims go up, and vacancies go up you need to pay attention. When you start hearing excuses for you team, "We overbuilt the market" or "Nothing we can do," you need to pay close attention. Those conditions may be true, but if your quality is below that of your competitors, you may be in trouble. Another one you may hear is that there are no employees, but think about that a minute. My guess is that there are enough employees in the market to fill your building, even if there are not enough to fill everyone's! Perhaps these issues were enhanced by a poor business decision when you decided to purchase or build the community. Many developers have built buildings that are functionally obsolete when they open. When that happens, you are now playing ball starting in the ninth inning and down five runs—not impossible, but damn hard to recover to win.

QUALITY GROWTH CURVE (QGC) - UNLIMITED POTENTIAL

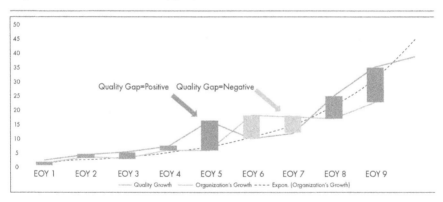

This does not represent actual data but is made for demonstration purposes only.

The Cycle and Seasons of Quality

In agriculture, the growing cycle is known, but the weather is only forecasted. Ancient principles and lessons guide farmers year after year. You prepare the ground—dirty, hard work that does not produce any immediate results. You have to have a lot of knowledge and faith that what you plant will produce, or you would never undertake the long-term approach to farming. Selecting seed comes next as you place more investments in the dark, cold ground, again a step that produces no immediate gratification or results. The next step does not produce any fruit either, but the budding plants rise from the ground, giving you hope. In this phase you are nurturing, protecting, and feeding the delicate plants. The final phase is the shortest in duration—the last step at the end when you get to harvest and be rewarded. But this last step is also the start of the next step, as the growth cycle repeats. Growing Cultures of Promise are similar. The causal loop of quality starts with investments into your operational infrastructure, which includes people and building relationships; as you plant the seeds, your employees', strategies', reputation's, and systems' success are not guaranteed.

In fact, it takes years to build teams of people and systems. If planted correctly, those investments start attracting customers who come to you not for your buildings but for the quality of your operations and employees. Those relationships are your crops. As they grow, just like in farming you have to nurture and protect them. Weeding your reputation is as constant as weeding your garden. It is tedious work where every interaction with your customers, your employees, your vendors, your partners, your regulators, and the general public perception is important. No relational detail is too small to ignore. No gap in quality is unimportant. When, not if, you make a mistake and mess up your promise to your customers, you must fix it, no matter the cost. If you don't pull the weed out of the field, it will grow—and at a faster pace than your quality can grow. And just like in your garden at home, that weed will produce seeds, and those seeds will further contaminate and negatively impact your crop.

As your quality grows, you will start to see the financial returns—your crop will be harvested. Your next step must be to take a portion of those returns and reinvest back into your organizational structure. As you do that, you will complete a healthy organizational cycle that will produce more employees, more residents, more buildings, and more financial returns that will fuel a natural growth of your organization.

CREATING AN EXCESS GROWTH CAPACITY (POSITIVE QUALITY GAP)

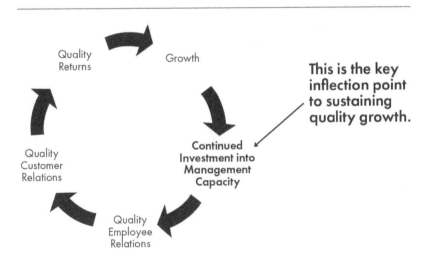

Or, when the quality gap is negative, pull back on the growth throttle and focus on building quality and leadership capacity. Organizations that fail often interrupt this natural cycle and outgrow their quality. They don't allow their roots to grow deep enough to carry the weight of the plant above the ground, or in our metaphor on leadership, they don't clean their springs, which erodes the quality experience of other stakeholders. Causes could be lack of investment into the operational infrastructure, allowing weeds to grow by not paying attention, or not understanding what invasive species look like and how to deal with them. Hiring the wrong people or keeping leaders in your organization who do not prioritize relationships over processes are good examples. Leadership that understands how to clean your springs and improve your springs can prevent these organic contaminants from taking root.

However, organizations can also fail by simply not knowing what they are doing. Mother Nature will not come to your aid if you plant the wrong crop in the wrong environment. We see this when national companies go into provincial markets without understanding the local culture. This is one of the reasons regional focused organizations are popular investment targets right now—they understand the local cultures, because all business is local. Failure can also occur by having poor strategy. Poor strategy can come in many different shapes and sizes. Selecting a capital partner that is not aligned with the long-term approach to achieving quality is one of the worst things you can do. They may not understand the business principles in this book. Or they may need you for just a short time because they plan to manage themselves at some point. Short-term management contracts and leases are dangerous if you want to build to long-term success. It is like planting a seed in the sand before a rainstorm. Or, failure can occur because of natural disasters, like COVID-19. In this case, there may not be anything you can do other than prepare, grow roots deep, and plan for the unexpected. The question is, when your organization outgrows its quality, are you willing to make the decisions to turn a negative quality gap into a positive quality gap?

QGC DECLINE CASUAL LOOP

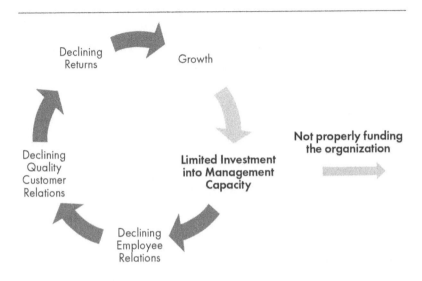

Building Operational Infrastructure

The answer to how to build our operational infrastructure may be right in front of us. When we build buildings, we set aside dollars to reinvest back into those physical plants. Called CAPX, or capital expenditures, dollars are budgeted or even managed by leaders to be put into a sinking fund, money set aside to be used for improvements to the property. Dollars are either designated for capital improvement deficiency or capital improvement repositioning. Both classes are important. Deficiency investment is done to bring a property up to current standards. Say your roof has been neglected, and it is starting to leak and cause money to be spent on repairs. Deficiency CAPX improvements would replace the roof to mitigate the growing expense impact to the operating statement and to ensure your residents are not inconvenienced due to roof leaks. Improvement CAPX spending is different. Improvement CAPX investments are used to reposition the property or alter the physical plant that will lead to more top-line revenue growth. An example could be to take out an unused multipurpose room and add a wellness clinic that would provide space for therapy or clinic rooms. Such an improvement would not only offer residents a benefit but would allow the community to tap new revenue sources.

The question is this: Why don't we approach investing in our organizations the same way as we invest in our real estate? Many operators are behind on investments into systems like IT infrastructure. The systems they use are dated and not able to handle the needs for increased reporting requirements, security, or access by employees and equity providers. Other improvement CAPX investments are needed into the IT backbone for the purpose of tapping healthcare collaborations and producing additional resources.

Infrastructure investments are not just physical. Organizations build on a solid foundation and also invest into strategy, people, and communications. Patience and timing are key ingredients to achieving quality. Every recipe has different ingredients, but every recipe, no matter the ethnicity, has one common element: time. Simply having all the ingredients and throwing them in a bowl is not enough to create great food, nor is it enough to create good teams and good outcomes. Cooking when you are hungry can lead to rushing the job and not getting a great dish, just like growing or scaling when you are too hungry for success can lead to undesirable outcomes.

It's not that you have to cook just for a few folks. We know that great food can be executed on a large scale, but we also know how difficult that is. The sample concept applies here. When you grow according to the QGC principles, you have to consider different means and methods at different stages of your organization's growth. Thinking that you can do things the same as when you had one, ten, or twenty buildings is organizational ignorance. Try to apply the same principles over a hundred buildings, and you may find yourself in a tight spot.

One simple way of gauging your infrastructure capacity is to ask yourself this question: "Are we delivering on our 3D Vision Framework promises consistently, or are we focusing on just our investors and ourselves, thinking that we will sort out the employee thing and the customer thing later—after we get big?" When you are a smaller organization—say, twenty buildings or less—you have the ability to do this by going around and looking at some key numbers. When you grow bigger, one or two people will never be able to keep their pulse on their promise fulfillment rate unless they build the infrastructure to measure their quality, which is the same as measuring their ability to fulfill their 3D promises.

Nothing in nature is stagnant for long, and if it is, it dies.

All organizations must plan to grow or plan to transition by merging, selling, or shutting their lights off. Applying the QGC principles will help you think of your business strategically. Because of the Boomer cohort, the future is bright, and this concept has never been more important as we prepare for one of the greatest business opportunities of a generation.

Create a possible quality gap now and grow.

KEY TAKEAWAYS:

- Uncontrolled pursuit of growth often compromises quality and promise fulfillment to residents and other stakeholders. Regional providers often outperform large national providers.

- Quality should be measured holistically across relationships, work/service delivery, and individual growth. Compliance metrics alone are insufficient.

- Creating a positive quality gap between growth rate and quality capacity enables responsible expansion. However, brief periods of negative quality gaps are sometimes necessary to reach full potential.

- Getting quality right is like agriculture—long cycles of cultivation building infrastructure before yields. Staying power and resilience matter more than speed.

- Different growth stages require recalibrated approaches. Small startups manage differently than mature regional players. No one formula applies all the time.

CHAPTER 12

The Promise: A Vision Forward

What is a promise?

A promise is when we give our word that we will *definitely* fulfill a personal assurance that we will do something.

For me, that promise I made to my grandmother Lillian all those years ago still lives and breathes. The future is guided by the lessons of the past. Listening to the pleadings of our family members and our friends not to put them in an old folks' home, we can hear the call toward a new way, a future way. Lax-ayxpa's healing waters had cared for the old ones of the Cayuse for unknown generations before it became Lehman Hot Springs. Like a seed of the great ponderosa pines that guard the waters today, those seeds germinating in the ground will not be denied. They will emerge once again in time to tower above all the other trees. The ancient circle continues, as Lehman Hot Springs has returned to its roots to be an example of how to care for each other, not just in our older years but in every stage of life.

The Great Boom Ahead

The natural forces of aging demographics, a pandemic, and a shrinking workforce have collided, creating a dynamic and impactful moment in history. Like the supercollider forcing these parts together, history has created an accelerated opportunity to change senior housing and care, long-term care, and healthcare for older adults. Seventy-three million American baby boomers are waiting for us to change the world. Technology, healthcare, and exploding public budgets can be a catalyst in a postpandemic era to make meaningful change. Never before have so many counted on so few to deliver on a simple promise—to take care of them.

The industry is emerging from the ashes of COVID-19 and a public that is unsure if it can trust it to deliver on an acceptable level of quality. Solutions like artificial intelligence, technology, healthcare integration, operational infrastructure investments, and policy, including meaningful immigration reform, must be part of the solution through strategy and innovation. But all these factors are not as important as making sure operators and capital investors understand what business they are in. Our promise cannot be fulfilled until we understand that this culture of promise must be approached differently from other businesses that have different promises.

Understanding for Capital and Operations

If I could write about only one thing in this book that I think would make the most difference for seventy-three-million-plus people, it would be about the cultural misunderstandings between capital and operations. Operators need to understand the needs and characteristics of our partners providing capital, and capital needs to understand our messy but hopeful culture of promise. If we can work through the differences between aspirational promises to our residents and families and our business promises to our employees and investors, we have the opportunity to not only fulfill both these types of promises but create environments for everyone to thrive.

We must do a better job of selecting capital partners who understand and can support our industry culture and leaders who know how to fulfill a business's promises and take care of people. Typically, the relationship between an operator and a capital provider, whether it is a seed capital investor, a group of friends and family, or public or private institutional capital, starts in the good times. However, partners should not be picked for how they behave when times are good but rather when times are challenging. Everyone is happy when you are making money, but when, not if, that changes in a relationship, how will the other party behave? Are all parties truly committed to playing the long game? The long game is creating quality first, then revenues, and finally a strong bottom line. Don't lead with sales; lead with quality, and you won't have to worry about sales.

You will go through periods of time like 9/11, the Great Financial Crisis, and COVID-19. When I started my company in 1996, I received a good piece of advice from a man named Tom Harrington. Tom said, "Fee, most people spend 90 percent of their time raising money to do a deal and then only 10 percent of their time spending it." He advised, "Do the opposite. Spend 90 percent of your time finding the right deal, and then you will only have to spend 10 percent of your time raising the money." Translated, this means that when you run a good business, the money will find you.

Operators, stop villainizing your capital providers. You took their money! Now you have a business promise that must be fulfilled all while you must fulfill your aspirational promise to your customers. Just like my grandpa Fancho distilled his whiskey, you need to distill your investors. Don't take money from people just because they can write a check! Take the 3D approach to align the values of your customers, your employees, and your investors. Values are your common denominator. Operators need to get smart and stop taking capital from any investor. You are the guardians of the galaxy, and by selecting the wrong capital, you endanger not only yourself but those you promise to care for—your residents and their employees.

Capital providers, you don't get a pass. Stop investing in a business that you don't understand. You have a responsibility to know what a culture of promise business requires and to select the right people to invest in. You hire too many operators that you like because they are like you. They are directive leaders who treat their business like they are stamping out widgets. I recommend reading Bill Schneider's book to understand the industry culture to invest in.

I see institutional investors entering the operating business and applying the same leadership style and philosophy that made them successful in running a financial institution. I think many of them will fail. You incentivize your deal people for closing deals; instead, you should be incentivizing outcomes for the customer. I get that plenty of money has been made by investors on deals that do not fulfill their promises in a 3D way, meaning the employees and customers win too. That is a win-lose, as Stephen Covey puts it. This will likely not stop unless the people making the investment decisions understand who to invest in, not just what real estate to invest in.

I believe many operators and capital providers are doing it right—but that is not enough. As an industry, we are known by our weakest link.

Some capital providers see operators as a necessary evil to get the returns they are looking for. Many operators wish they could click their heels together and make analysts disappear for good. But neither is possible, and we are stuck with each other to find common ground on how to fulfill our promises to our customers, older adults, employees, and our investors.

I used to think that it would be the operators who were going to be the ones to create the change in quality for senior housing and care. I don't anymore. Instead, *it's the capital that will lead the way by making sure they are investing in operators that support people with strategy, innovation, and infrastructure, not just real estate.* Perhaps operators will be the ones in the future to deploy the capital. Perhaps the lines between the real estate capital and operators will merge and we will invest in entire enterprises that focus on one thing, the quality between the customer and the frontline employee. A new type of organization will emerge, much like in other industries, where the capital will be in service to all the components of the business that, in turn, will serve the fulfillment of both promises.

"They that have the gold rule" is actually true for the moment. But in this profession, failure to achieve quality for your customers, and that gold will find itself in the hands of those who can. If we are really going to impact the quality, it will take capital to make it happen. Therefore, *my new golden rule says that those who take care of folks well will eventually get the gold.*

When capital realizes, not just gives lip service to, that we are investing and caring for people, not stamping out widgets on an assembly line, and choose to invest in organizations that take that 3D approach, you will start to see changes. When capital providers invest in the operational infrastructure and people, and stop funding companies that treat this profession like another real estate play like any other fast-food rollout or hotel chain, you will start to see quality flourish. But saying the right things is not enough; you have to believe it, and the proof lies in what actually happens between each person we care for and our frontline workers.

Much is being discussed about capital for operations. Entire industries and work groups are debating and discussing how to fund operations. An underlying assumption that there is no capital for operations seems to permeate the national conferences. I disagree. If you have good strategy and structure your organization correctly, plenty of capital is available. Many operators who took management contracts and leases seem to be the ones that find themselves undercapitalized in the operations. Others have done exceptionally well by making sure the capital stack is fully integrated by taking part in the development fees and the promoted interest in the real estate. The problem is, that approach worked well prior to the sharp rise in interest rates, and today I am not sure enough overall compensation exists in each transaction. Discussions need to happen on how to invest into operations in the current real estate-challenged world. Perhaps new financial vehicles need to be developed? I believe so, but I also believe the following four key points of view must be considered in any evolution:

- Capital cannot access the financial resources of the people who live in the communities except through the operators.

- The opportunity is in creating places people "want to" live and can afford to live.

- In communities where people "have to" move to, we should set the same expectation of quality as in the communities where they "want to." Quality isn't about how fancy the building is or how many food choices there are; it's about the relationships, the work, and the employees.

- To create places people "want to" live takes investing in infrastructure to deliver on the promises to all the stakeholders.

Take as an example the way residential real estate developers build subdivisions. They buy a big piece of land and then put in roads, sewer systems, storm water systems, and other utilities way before a single home is built. Capital and operators would be well advised to take a page out of their playbook and do the same. Operators must invest and create the infrastructure for operational support long before they build a community for people to live in. They also must do this in a way that supports the different business cultures between capital and operators. Anyone can call themselves an operator, just like anyone can call themselves capital. It doesn't matter what you say you are; it matters what you do. What qualifies an individual or an organization as an operator is not their self-proclamation but their experience, their understanding, their passion, and their actions. Invest in operators that understand how to produce quality at the point of contact with the customer and how to fulfill their business promises. These people lead with quality, not money, as their purpose. My guess is that many will start saying and doing the right things in the near future as the path becomes clear. The key is to know the difference between those who are just talking about quality and who can deliver on quality.

Most of us like things to be neatly packaged and predictable. Senior housing operations are not simple or clean—they are messy, like farmers who get dirty when they plant a crop in a field. Capital must find a way to allow the messiness of fulfilling a subjective promise of taking care of people and not try to put operators into a neat and tidy box. I know that freshly minted MBAs and CEOs from other industries with different cultures think they will come in and clean that all up with rigidty with procedures and policies, like a precision military operation, but they won't. It can and must be improved, but it must be done with the understanding that our industry is an enrichment enterprise, as Bill Schneider describes. You cannot change the industry's culture, but you can build better systems inside its principles. When both groups understand each other's needs and spend the time to really create a thoughtful strategy, I believe ways of investing dollars into operations will emerge. Our profession is evolving, but the industry can never deviate from our promise to take care of people.

Failure will happen if the only goal of rigidity is to eliminate human judgement. In a culture of promise, human judgment is what enhances experience of the customer. If the aim of the corporate structure is to enhance human judgment, it will succeed, but if it's solely focused on maximizing financial returns over a short period of time, the results may not be as good as hoped for.

Capital and operators need to play the long game by starting right, thinking about our own homes. We all have families, and we all will need support as older adults. Our youth will someday be gone, and we can no longer put off the realization that our days are limited and that *we are our future customers.* My grandmother used to say that every year goes faster and faster as you age. We cling to our younger selves, denying, procrastinating, and hoping while time accelerates. To prevent ourselves from living in an "old folks' home," what can we do to create environments and help people squeeze everything they can out of that chapter of life?

Whether you work in capital or in operations, my vision is that you make an aspirational promise to yourself and your profession. We can improve, but it takes time. Promise to make progress over the last year, then make progress over the following year and the following by using all your powers and resources focused on one thing: creating quality for all by fulfilling that promise. Be passionate, visionary, vulnerable, and commit to serving your fellow man. Make a difference by saying what you see and being brave. It's not someone else's job to make things better or to make your life better—it's yours. Promise to make money as a by-product that follows fulfilling your promise, like the apples you get after you plant and nurture an orchard.

Research, Innovation, and Strategy

Three pillars of our path forward as an industry are research, innovation, and strategy. We need all three to fulfill our promise.

Researching Our Promise

Now is the time for us to answer some questions with a high degree of certainty. Leaders must use data and research to answer the question of why we have such vast variances in performance and quality in senior housing at a time when we have record numbers of customers entering the market. It's in each of our personal self-interests to set aside an ideology that keeps producing the same results and be willing to ask, "Why?" The stakes are too high for us not to get this right. How can we promise to take care of anyone if we won't genuinely ask what they want and need?

In addition, not only is the size of the market growing; we have a declining workforce. Government budgets are competing for priorities, and healthcare costs continue to soar. COVID-19 offers us the data and opportunity to study public policy's impact on the safety and well-being of stakeholders, including the customers, the employees, and even capital. One question to include is the following: What are the root causes of quality differences among regions, operators, and types of care? You can hire anthropologists and consultants, write grants, and crunch data to help lead the way forward. We need to understand why and listen to visionary researchers like Bill Schneider who offer clues to how we can change the future.

As I write this book, trade groups are working to evolve the industry through a quality data initiative. Looking for a consensus to measure our quality and value to our customer is a must to the maturation of our profession. If we do not take care of our own house-keeping, someone else will, and that someone works in Washington, DC. We must be willing to be vulnerable to the truth by including our customers in the discussion. What our customers think of us matters and must be the cornerstone that we navigate, compare, and correlate to other data, or in my opinion we will fail. If we collect data only for the purpose of trying to prove that what we do is of value versus collecting data so we can accurately see where our quality gaps and limiters are, all will be lost.

A Promise to Innovate

Let's make a promise to innovate for the future, to focus on the grand aspirational promise to take care of our customers, our families, and each other. Let's promise to focus on growing our quality as enthusi-astically as we have focused on growing our number of buildings, our revenues, and our profit margins. *Not because margin is not important but because margin is important.* And the belief that when you do the right thing for your employees and customers, and *if* you make good strategic decisions, the rising tide will lift all the boats.

We need to innovate as an industry and as individual organiza-tions to create the solutions and living environments that will enrich their lives. Innovations rise up from the ground level, like a spring. Those innovations won't come from a bunch of executives sitting around a conference room table; they will come from the front line.

But if we don't invest in our operational infrastructure, our teams won't have the space to innovate because they are always working short. Developing a culture that promotes ideas to get better and innovate in our own organizations and our industry will allow us to improve quality outcomes and change with our customer base. Setting up continuous improvement systems to change with the people we serve will keep our organizations relevant and sustainable.

Invest in Strategy

Love is not enough, nor is just being innovative. You actually have to *&%$-ing do something! Organizations must also have a solid strategy. I believe the state of the senior housing and care industry is in a similar spot as the auto industry was in the 1970s and 1980s. The US auto industry was in trouble; it became complacent and overconfident and was getting innovated out of business by new entrants like Datsun, Nissan, and Honda. The new just-in-time concepts helped reduce costs and deliver products that customers actually wanted instead of what Henry Ford told them they should want. The oil embargo and rising gas prices caused the US consumer to embrace a more fuel-efficient car as well as the innovative designs that were more pleasing to the customer. This is not unlike COVID-19 causing our customers to reject many of the housing options offered today. Rising housing and healthcare costs are necessitating innovation in our sector. Finding ways for senior housing and healthcare organizations to cooperate can not only stretch our financial resources but build better environments with more resources for our workforces and create communities folks cannot wait to get old enough to move into and staff cannot wait to work in.

The generation of baby boomers is not going to accept the living environments and services of their parents' generation. Much has been written on this, so I don't need to go into it other than to say that boomers will want what they want when they want it. They will demand quality, and they will demand places to live, not places to go to die. This is the most outspoken generation in history, and just like when they burned their bras and rebelled against the Man, they will do the same with nursing homes, wheelchairs, and tapioca. To ignore them is to shipwreck upon the cliffs of humanity.

Much work has been completed on strategy recently, so I won't reinvent the wheel here. The strategy I am most familiar with as the current vice chair for strategy is that of the National Investment Center's strategic direction for our industry.

I agree with so much of their approach. But I will also add that every organization must consider environmental, social, and governance criteria (ESG) in their strategic consideration. This is where I may lose some of the folks I grew up with who believe that climate change, governance, and our social responsibility is irrelevant. I firmly believe it is not. In brief, ESG is simply about considering a 360-degree view (just like the 3D view I have been touting) of the risks your organizational stakeholders face.

If organizations do not consider the costs of building and operating in climate-affected areas, they will never be able to fulfill their promise for financial returns or be able to take care of people. Whether you deal with the health impacts of forest fires, hurricanes, or earthquakes, you must have plans and then account for the financial impacts of those plans. It's just smart. I say this as a man raised in a family tied very specifically to the land we lived on.

If you fail to plan for social risks and the groundswell of social change around diversity, equity, and inclusion (DEI), you will alienate and isolate your organization from the already-slim workforce. If you do not consider the risks to your organizational governance with succession planning, investor influences, and political and bureaucratic impacts, you are not running a business—you are gambling. Each organization will need to adapt its own strategy, and the one thing I can tell you is that you will need to do it differently than you did it before COVID-19.

Start with Your Workforce

Lack of understanding between operators and capital is just one of the gaps that limit our quality. The other is with the workforce itself. Like the military, every organization has officers and enlisted. Understanding that they come from different perspectives and speak different languages is one of the most important points of view needed to improve our quality. In an inverted hierarchy, the frontline workers directly support the customers, and the managers by necessity must support the front line. Simply inverting your org chart will allow you to think and act differently.

For example, workplace stability[8] should be at the top of every organization's strategy; it is number one. This includes providing all the resources that our workforce needs. It includes working with our state and local governments and, yes, unions to the extent that they can help us effectively deliver on our promise. As labor shortages affect every industry from supply chain to hospitality, our own industry is not immune. Immigration and recruiting from offshore cultures of care must be a priority for those of us in senior housing and care.

---

8   Ruth K Weirich, Workplace Stability (Highlands, Tx.: aha! Process, 2016).

America's relative prosperity and opportunities still make us a desirable country for people to work and live. Remember the bear theory? This can give us significant advantages in labor, but that alone cannot replace the growing gaps.

COVID-19 has created a great schism in quality, a fork in the road. Some companies have fully recovered while others are struggling to keep their noses above water or are currently holding their breath, as they have descended below the waterline of financial viability. It is unlikely that low interest rates will return in time to save these overleveraged and underperforming organizations. Only by redirecting our strategy to take care of our workforce and customers can we improve and move forward and fulfill our promises.

A Promise to Our Workforce

The only way we can fulfill our promises to our customers is by fulfilling our promises to our stakeholders, too, and our employees are the gateway to accomplishing this. I would contend that we need to examine our strategy and systems to understand and innovate around being great employers. We need to think of our employees with the same level of attention we give our customers and investors.

The 3D methodology I've advocated throughout this book can help you do that. We cannot fulfill our promises with disastrously high employee turnover rates. Some indications are that for frontline staff, it's 70 to 150 percent—or more! (Those are horrifying numbers.) Not only is that hard on budgets, coworkers, and managers; it's devastating to the families who live and engage in our communities. Just when a resident and their family get to know a caregiver, they are gone.

This labor issue is a complex subject that likely needs an entire book to itself, but I bring it up now to demonstrate how important the concept of an aspirational promise is. Many of our employees quit because they feel they simply cannot do a good enough job. They feel they are always letting the residents and families down. Their managers sometimes can be pejorative and push blame, making the job just not worth the money. And, of course, there is always the money. No one disagrees that caregivers should make more money. The problem is that neither do people want to pay more for care. Public and private concerns constantly fight to keep the prices down while pushing for higher employee compensation and regulations. These two things cannot coexist. Our workforce problems need to be solved with more than just salary. We must create workplace stability through understanding, connection, and resources.

The concept of aspirational promises is critical to our industry because it frames the reality for workers and customers that perfection is a mirage, and it explains that the only failure is by not solving the problems when they occur. What is most important is that when we break an aspirational promise, it requires us to fix the problem and make it right. Government regulators should measure how we resolve problems, not solely report when we have problems. Unrealistic expectations for our organizations to prevent people from the challenges of aging do not help. Rather, regulators should consider how we deal with and resolve the problems. Simply reporting to the public that someone was injured creates a false narrative and hurts the community, the organization, and the public themselves. The balance between aspirational promises and business promises offers residents and workers alike clarity and context, and if we have clarity, we can do amazing things.

When I started the company, I had no idea what I was doing or what I was getting into. I thought it seemed easy enough. I held on to a promise made with everything I had. You can never stop improving and fixing problems—and back then we had more problems than fixes. For example, you can never understand employees' perspectives in long-term care until you work there; you can never understand the customers' perspectives until you have family who live there.

Until we innovate to attract, retain, and offer lifelong career paths, we will not make any meaningful progress toward quality and fulfilling our promise. Our leadership and our frontline employees speak two different languages and need two different support structures. One may be the language of empaths ... the other, the language of numbers and bottom lines. The government cannot be the sole advocate for our workforce, nor will unions be the solution. We have to internally advocate for our employees, build systems of trust, and create career path opportunities, like being a lifetime caregiver, a noble and worthy career.

Beyond any doubt is a true need for all stakeholders in our industry to work together and focus on the outcome in a 3D way, understanding that when everyone wins, we all win. We must have more than love; we must have vision and strategy and be well capitalized to fulfill our promises to all our stakeholders.

"Pulling yourself up by the bootstraps" is a concept I am sure you are familiar with if you had a parent, grandparent, coach, or older mentor. It's a concept that assumes we have executive functioning thinking to help us get through the tough patches in life. The only problem is that a significant portion of our workforce doesn't have straps on their boots or even any boots. Let's face it—in the past, our sector, our industry, our profession has been built on the shoulders of a workforce with few other options for jobs. For our workforce, it's often a choice between fast-food jobs or senior living. The concepts in this book point us to the important limiter to quality in our sector, our entry-level workforce, and the limiter of our entry-level workforce are the managers and leaders who support them.

We need to put our workforce at top priority because they are the ones who actually take care of our customers. Taking care of the workforce is on the minds of every viable organization today, especially postpandemic, when employees became hard to find.

Capitalism gives us the freedom to take care of our customers and employees, not just the investors. However, as in the book *The Lord of the Rings,* if you put the ring on, all the power goes to your head, corrupting yourself and enslaving others. It just gives people the power to pursue their values. Money amplifies the values of those who direct it. Contrary to some current rhetoric, I believe money and capitalism are not inherently evil on their own but the vehicle to make change.

I know this line of thinking might sound adolescent for some MBA types, but stay with me here. Capitalism gives us the freedom to do good. Bilbo, because of his values and worldview, knew it was corrupting. He felt it could corrupt and pulled himself from its grasp to leave the world a better place. My point is that capitalism has the power to do good just as much as bad. It just depends on whose hand the ring is worn. Don't throw Bilbo out with the bathwater, to rephrase an old saying my grandma used to espouse.

Bridging the Divide: Federal, State, and Local Governments

This is a team sport, and our public servants play an important role on the team. After all, we share a mutual goal of providing the best care for older adults. However, far too often it feels we are not on the same team with the same goals. Regulatory departments tell us that we cannot fail, and if we do, we will be fined and our "failings" publicly displayed. I don't disagree that organizations, both for profit and not for profit, should be called out for poor performance when they take the public's money or abuse its trust, but the problem is that the reporting often does not tell the accurate story. Definitions for abuse and other indicators they report are broad and not always evenly applied. Giving an accurate picture to the public is vital and should be compared to what would happen in the home if our housing and services did not exist.

We all must remember that we are making aspirational promises here. We will fail, people will fall, and people will pass away. When that happens, the current go-to solution is to make more regulations and requirements. Overregulation restricts the operators' ability to solve problems and raises the cost of solving those problems. Ultimately those costs get passed on to the very people we are trying to care for and impacts those loved ones helping to pay—both public and private payers. My hope is that we can see each other as important parts of the same team, inviting two-way problem-solving conversations that actually solve the problem and make it better. To not do this will mean declining quality and more expensive quality, and it will limit the providers, driving the smaller providers out of business and aggregating care into only the largest organizations. We will always have bad actors that come and go, but to punish all organizations is not the right solution. The vast majority of organizations are working to do the right thing. We can do better together.

Bridging the Divide: Mutual Promises of Capital and Operators

Soon you, too, will be eighty-five years old and looking to move into a The Springs Living community or another retirement community somewhere in the country so you can squeeze every bit of quality life out of this ride. If it's a The Springs Living community, don't move in and expect to just wait to die. We will push you to contribute, to laugh, and to give of yourself so that your last breaths breathe no regret. Isolated alone in a single-family home may be your choice, but sharing life, even a new and scary chapter, can make all the difference.

I know this is a business book, so some of you might be sighing a big *ugh* right now. No matter. I am being vulnerable in hopes that it will set off a chain reaction like others have done for me. I believe success is so much more than making money and is found in giving what you have to someone else, words from the Randy Travis song "A Satisfied Mind," in a way that creates its own success for you too. Your story is important and impactful, and you can make some difference and leave your corner of the world better than you found it. That place is one where everyone's fortunes rise, not just those of the CEO and the shareholders. Dedicate yourself to the saying "a rising tide lifts all boats." If each of us made the places in our life just a little bit better, the world would benefit.

If you are in the arena, you have also made a promise to someone or something. Just by showing up, you have an implicit promise to all stakeholders and, most importantly, yourself. The question is this: Will you embrace it as a promise or treat it as a job? I have been creating environments to care for older adults for almost thirty years. The one universal recommendation over all these years from generations of our customers is to live now. Don't wait to live, love, and make a difference—the time is now.

We opened The Springs at Missoula in December of 2004. This was our prototype of a concept that contained independent living, assisted living, and memory care all under one roof. Not only was this our first out-of-market community, making us a regional company when it opened, but it was large even for a Class A or B market at the time, and here we were building it in a town that had less than about fifty thousand people. This was the first community purposefully built using the metaphor of Lehman Hot Springs, with three levels of continuum the way my grandfather had built the lodge, cabins, and campground at The Springs. When we cut the ribbon at the grand opening, I knew it would not take long for us to tell if this new prototype was going to work in any market, much less a tertiary one. In our pub we hung a picture that hangs in my office today. It is of a cowboy pointing in one direction with the caption, "This is the place!"

Excited to finish the manuscript for A Culture of Promise.

Just like all those years ago, today I am drawn to this Wild West image, but if I could change the caption, I would say, "This is the time!"

Promise of Gold

I looked across the basketball court during halftime at the high school boys and girls state basketball championships in Pendleton, Oregon, in 2013. On the other side of the court, I noticed an old acquaintance I'd known when I was a boy. Jesse Jones Jr. was one of the last full-blooded Cayuse Native Americans alive and chief of the tribe. It had been many years since I had seen him last. As I focused my sight to make sure it was really him, a vision of teepees popped into my head, the way an image in a stereograph suddenly emerges when you stop straining to find the picture hidden inside. My grandma had told me this story, but I hadn't thought of it in years. I strolled around the court and grabbed the empty seat behind the score table where Jesse was a fixture. As I stuck out my hand and reintroduced myself, his big smile connected me to my past.

The pleasantries completed, I pressed him on the story. "Jesse, my grandma used to tell me of a tribe that would come to Lehman in the summer with their teepees. She said they had a gold mine at Lehman. Do you know what tribe that was?"

He cocked his head as if to shake a forgotten memory loose and said, "They would have been from our tribe, the Cayuse."

"OK, then," I said, having set him up for the real ask. "Can you give me the GPS coordinates for the lost gold mine, since I just bought Lehman again?" I said it in jest but partly in hope.

He looked puzzled. "There's no lost gold mine that I have ever heard of," he said with a finality that extinguished that boyhood dream of my past. I had spent many summers wandering the hills and canyons of Lehman, looking, hoping for that chance discovery that would bring all the wealth of a discovered treasure and ease the constant financial struggle our family lived with. If I could just find that gold mine, we could fix the pool and buy a new pickup to replace the beaten-up, rusty green Ford. Like the first time I heard there was no Santa Claus, Jesse's verification was the breath that blew out the candle of finding the gold mine.

But then he continued, and his next words took my breath away.

"That was our retirement community," he said with an intonation that I recognized as truth.

"Did you just say it was your tribe's retirement community?" I replied, trying to absorb the meaning.

"Yes, it's where we would take our old ones, to soak in the water and feel better. The waters would heal them of bone disease, arthritis, and make them feel younger."

The story continued for a number of minutes while I sat trying to process what I was hearing. The Cayuse people had a winter camp above the town of Pilot Rock, up McKay Creek and just over the ridge from Lehman. In the spring of each year, a group of younger tribal members would take all the older members south, through the "hole in the wall," a narrow gap in the rock just wide enough for a horse and a person, offering the only gradual passage up the steep mountain and toward Lehman Hot Springs. "Once there, they would bathe in the hot healing waters and feel better and younger for a while."

As I sat listening, his story connected the dots of my story. His story healed the wounds of my past with the same unseen power of the body to heal a cut. But it did more than that; it made me feel small. Not small in a negative way but small in an infinitely large way. I felt like a pawn on the chessboard of the universe, insignificant on my own but, when moved by the invisible hand of the universe, a part of destiny itself. You see, Jesse didn't know what I did for a living. He didn't know about my promise to my grandmother all those years ago, and he didn't know that for the last seventeen years I had built an organization that dedicated itself to taking care of the old ones. And, like he didn't know, I didn't know the place where I was born and grew up had always been a retirement community. Unknowingly, he had just placed the last piece of the puzzle, completing the reason for why I'd made the promise. It all made sense now.

All those dark, hard years, I had thought I had created The Springs Living with bare hands, ideas, risks, and a lot of love and hard work from those who shared the vision. I thought I was just fulfilling a promise to my grandmother, but in an instant, I realized that I was a part of something bigger that bridged time, peoples, and infinitely diverse cultures. I realized that now I was part of something that was fulfilling a promise to everyone's grandmothers and grandfathers. All the coincidences that had happened over the years and along the way now seemed guided. The trip to the nursing home in Mission, the promise to my grandmother, the chance meeting with Tom Clark on top of the Peachtree in Atlanta, the starfish along the beach were just a few.

But what happened in the past throughout this story, while inspiring, is not the point of this book. The point of this book is what we can do with the future. You are reading this book because you, as I have been, are also a part of an invisible force working to make the world better. Whatever corner of the world, or type of organization in whatever industry, through your unique story, your knowledge, skills, and abilities, and your values, you can make all the difference. I promise.

The end of this book is just the beginning. Thank you for reading.

–Fee

KEY TAKEAWAYS:

- Innovation must be grounded in frontline worker and resident needs and perspectives, not just top-down visions. Their ideas will transform the industry.

- Don't lead with sales. Lead with quality and you won't have to worry about sales.

- Operators must understand the needs and characteristics of their captial partners BEFORE they take the investment.

- Understanding differences between operational and capital cultures is key. Neither is inherently good or bad, but balanced collaboration is essential.

- The employee experience defines the resident experience. Becoming an employer of choice through career development, etc. must be a priority.

- Partnerships between industry and regulators focused on constructive problem-solving and appropriate risk-taking, not just compliance, will advance quality.

EPILOGUE

Today, Lehman Hot Springs is owned by my family once again. I repurchased it in 2012 and reconnected it physically to our story. My quest to fulfill my promise also allowed me to make my dreams come true, and getting Lehman back in the family felt like righting a wrong. Since 1925, it had taken care of our family, and now it was time for us to take care of it. Like an organization that has been bled dry or a building with significant deferred maintenance, Lehman was not healthy when I got it back. I have been restoring it, nurturing it, and learning more of the secrets of this ancient place. Today, we take our leadership teams there to let them experience the story and feel the connection to the ancient people who once used it for the same thing we do today—to take care of the "old ones," just like Chief Jesse Jones described all those years ago. Each year, current and future leaders visit to learn firsthand how they are part of a great story and to learn the lessons the ancient springs provide. Our future plans may include making Lehman available to other organizations so they can experience this special place.

For generations, our family had looked to Lehman like the gold mine, panning its coins from visitors who wanted to soak just to make a living. It was a hard living to be had when it was operating as a resort.

While my family thought there was a lost gold mine, it turns out that the real gold was in the idea. For so long Lehman Hot Springs had struggled to take care of our family. Now it was our turn to take care of it. It was tired, worn out, and overused—it was like buying back your grandpa's old classic car that needed to be restored. Now, the springs can retire; it can rest and be restored. Our family is dedicated to restoring this ancient and sacred place. Its environmentally sensitive areas are thriving with what indigenous peoples call first foods, a limited resource that needs good stewardship. Our hope is that Lax-ayxpa will continue to be an example of how to care for people so they will feel better, for at least a while.

After all, this place is our story and it's our privilege to strive to transform the way people think, feel, and experience living as older adults.

ABOUT THE AUTHOR

Fancho Fee Stubblefield Jr. (Fee) is the founder and CEO of The Springs Living, LLC, a company he started in order to take care of his grandmother. That story is this book. Fee has attended Oral Roberts University and was a diver on its swim team before attending Clemson University. His entrepreneurial drive interrupted his planned academic path, and he never looked back. He grew up in Pendleton, Oregon, and at Lehman Hot Springs Resort, a small family-owned business near there. He is a pilot, cattle rancher, and entrepreneur. He lives with his life partner, Julie, married thirty-eight years, on a small farm in Amity, Oregon, where they raised three children: Matthew, Emma, and Jonathan. This is his first book.

Fee is currently serving or has served on several nonprofit boards, including as chair of the Providence Milwaukie Hospital Foundation, chair of the Oregon Healthcare Association, and currently services on the Board of Directors for the National Investment Center as its inaugural Vice Chair of Strategy.

ACKNOWLEDGMENTS

None rise alone. Over the years I have worked alongside thousands of people who have joined me at The Springs Living to make a difference and strive to leave the world a better place. Each of them has made a difference in my life and in those we serve; even if seemingly small, all contributions matter. Twenty-four seven, 365, we serve, never sleeping, never stopping, just like the springs at Lehman Hot Springs, so that we can be present for people in need. Building an organization that supports other people is truly a team sport. I am the lucky one who gets to be the storyteller of ideas, hard work, and love for their fellow man that we have learned together. Thank you team, coworkers, and colleagues.

To my family, children Matthew and Madi, Emma and Bryan, Jonathan and Jenna, my parents Fancho and Katie, and Julie's parents LTC Rodney and Dorthy Pimental, and especially to my life partner Julie who has spent countless hours collaborating on this book as well as life.

Thank you, Bob Kramer at the National Investment Center for Seniors Housing and Care. Your inspiration, vision, and appetite to be disruptive will be a legacy that makes life better for untold older adults.

I also want to acknowledge Jim Carlson and all of colleagues in the Oregon Healthcare Association. The Oregon Healthcare Association serves to build cooperation and understanding in the senior housing and care industry and to be a link between those who serve residents daily and the government that is granted responsibility by its citizens to oversee and care for our society.

And thanks to the folks at Forbes, who know how to get the best out of their writers and support those stories that must be told or be lost to history.

Nothing gets accomplished without capital, and I have had the privilege of support from strong and visionary investors like Greg Hemstreet, Harrison Street Real Estate, as well as friends and family who believed in our mission. Thank you.

And finally, I am deeply grateful that I was born and raised deep in the Blue Mountains of Oregon at a place called Lehman Hot Springs. Thank you to Lax-ayxpa for your inspiration.